TALKING PROUD

Rediscovering
the Magical Season
of the
1980 Buffalo Bills

TALKING PROUD

Rediscovering the Magical Season of the 1980 Buffalo Bills

Rich Blake

OCHIBI PRESS

Published by:
Ochibi Press
P.O. Box 84
Big Indian, NY 12410

ISBN: 978-0-9912622-0-5

Jacket design by Tony Zajkowski
Interior design and layout by Mulberry Tree Press, Inc.

Talking Proud is a work of non-fiction.

This book is dedicated to the diehards.

*"Buffalo's got a spirit
Talking proud, talking proud."*

—"We're Talking Proud" theme song
(Alden Schutte)

"We'll roll on with our heads held high."

—The Living End

Contents

Acknowledgments

The author wishes to thank the following for their contributions to the telling of this story: Doug Benge, Greg Bensel, Dan Blake, Patsy Blake, Shawn Blake, Thomas Blake, Jr., Mark Brammer, Terry Braunstein, Jerry Butler, Vic Carucci, Andrew Craig, Joe Cribbs, Joe DeLamilleure, Conrad Dobler, Pat Donlon, Matt Dwyer, Michael Dwyer, the Elias Sports Bureau, especially John Labombarda, Joe Ferguson, Therese Forton, John Gallivan, Teresa Giles, Tom Horton, Chris Keating, Rod Kush, Dennis Lynch and the Bills archives staff, Dan Manucci, Paul McLeary, Brian Milligan, Bill Munson, Louie Mustillo, Shane Nelson, Jeff Nixon, Larry Norton, Artie Ponto, Lou Piccone, Albert Reiss and the archivists at the Buffalo State Library, Jim Ritcher, Debra Rizzo, Isiah Robertson, Alden and Susan Schutte, Mike Shaw, William H. Siener and the staff of the Buffalo and Erie County Historical Society, Fred Smerlas, Kay Stephenson, Patricia Stewart, Megan Toohey, Tim Toohey, John Turney, Phil Villapiano, Matt Walsh, Ron Watson, and Tony Zajkowski.

A very special thanks to Meryl Kaye, without whose support, patience, feedback, editing, warmth and kindness this project would not have been possible.

Introduction

I grew up on the eastern fringe of South Buffalo, in West Seneca, not far from Lackawanna, right near the Abbott Road/Dorrance Avenue border and just a few miles from Ralph Wilson Stadium. It will always be Rich Stadium to me.

One of my earliest childhood recollections is of my father taking me to see the stadium out in Orchard Park while it was still under construction. Although I was barely four years old, a faint echo in my mind survives: a concrete sky, distant bulldozers, a mountain of mud.

My father, a railroad switchman and public school janitor who tore off a little extra income in the autumn taking tickets at the old War Memorial Stadium, insisted that the Bills were naming their new stadium after me and I believed him.

My single earliest memory of "the Bills," albeit a hazy one, was watching them on a portable black-and-white television stationed in my garage one rainy late summer night back in 1975. It was a pre-season game and Buffalo's gifted cornerback Robert James had suffered a catastrophic, career-ending knee injury. I only vaguely understood what was happening on the field but somehow the suddenness and cruelty of it all registered in the sparsely filled hard drive of my brain. James writhing in agony has stuck with me all these years.

My second Bills memory was watching them play on

Thanksgiving Day, 1976, against the Detroit Lions. That day O.J. Simpson ran for 273 yards, breaking the NFL single-game rushing mark of 250 yards, his record at the time. I can remember my father, my grandfather and a few of my uncles laughing in astonishment as Simpson ripped off 10-15-20 yards, play after play after play. I can still distinctly hear my Uncle Jimmy, a Vietnam vet, remark, "I could watch him run all day."

Huddled around my grandparents' Cheektowaga living room television set with the elders watching the Bills, it was all so exquisitely comfortable. The Bills lost 27–14 that Thanksgiving day, the eighth straight defeat in what would be a miserable 2–12 season.

I kept following. The Bills kept losing. At 8 years old, I'd played enough outdoor Cazenovia ice hockey to know that even the shittiest teams snuck away with a win every once in a while. It seemed incomprehensible that the Bills *always* lost.

A few weeks later, just before Christmas, I was sitting in my basement watching the Bills finish out a 4 P.M. game at Miami that seemed to last well into the December evening when down the stairs came my father's friend, a local politician named Chris Walsh. Mr. Walsh was a wonderfully gregarious character who in a long-running inside joke pretended to play wide receiver for the Bills (a third-round pick out of Notre Dame), only he was always sidelined with some new injury. "Well Richie, the doctors say that I could be back out there in a few more weeks," Mr. Walsh would say with comically feigned graveness. "If they need me I'll be ready." I recall him lurching his head down as he descended the stairs, asking for the score. The game clock was ticking down and the players had just started walking off the field, though I naively clung to the waning seconds. Not until it was finally over did I face up to yet another defeat. "They lost again," I grumbled, clearly one dejected little kid. "Why don't the Bills ever win?"

And I never forgot Chris Walsh, as if to mitigate the situation, reminding me it was the Dolphins that had beaten us and that "Buffalo can never beat these guys." At the time I took this to mean that the Dolphins beating the Bills was a rule, like how you always had to look both ways before you crossed the street.

I later realized my assessment was not that far off base.

My first trip to Rich Stadium—and sweet taste of Bills glory—would come the following season, on October 16, 1977. Several recollections of that experience are unmistakably locked away. I can tell you the outcome: 3–0, Bills over the Atlanta Falcons, still the lowest-scoring game in team history and at the time only the second 3–0 game played since the NFL/AFL merger in 1970.

My sister Patsy, eight years older than me and a junior at Mount Mercy Academy, took me to the game, along with my brother Shawn and one of her girlfriends. Later we met up with their boyfriends, a couple of skinny guys from Fort Erie, Ontario, both of them Kenny Loggins look-alikes and chain smokers of Kools. My 19-year-old brother Danny, an usher at the stadium, had set it all up, arranging for us to get in free through one of the ticket-takers he knew. It was a miserable day—windy and rainy. One of the smallest crowds in team history, barely 27,000, had shown up for this galactical showdown. It didn't matter to me—I was in heaven. I remember being bundled up, heavy wool blankets across our laps and a big thermos of hot chocolate at our feet. I just couldn't believe the whole time I was *actually* at a Bills game. The aroma, an even mix of beer, peanut shells and hot dogs, remains to this day mine for the conjuring.

You wouldn't think that sitting through a dreary late October afternoon surrounded by bearded Canadians all for one lousy second-quarter Neil O'Donoghue field goal would change my life. But it did.

I stood and watched breathlessly as the Falcons, late in the game, trailing 3–0, lined up on fourth down and one yard to go at the Bills' 4. Instead of trying to tie the game with a chip shot field goal the Falcons went for broke. Someone, everyone, shouted, "They're going for it!" and the murmuring crowd braced, and then, growing steadily louder, roared for the Falcons to dare. The Falcons' quarterback rolled out toward the sideline and sped for the easy first-down and then somehow, though I couldn't quite see what was happening, the Bills' secondary came all at once, swarming in a vintage Rich Stadium gang-tackle that poured out of bounds. The Bills had held!

It was a blur, even then, but as I bring myself back to that moment I can see the strangers, some of them drunken and wild-eyed, some of them reassuringly familiar-looking, all of them clapping and beaming. Our small point advantage remained intact. As a member of the crowd I realized that I had dibs on the exuberance. To think that I had never even experienced a Bills victory as a young football fan coming of age in the Jim Ringo era.

Well, that victory over the Falcons was the first time the Bills had won a game since October 3 *of the prior season*, a 14-game skid which solidified the national impression of the Bills as a team that "sucked."

But I was officially indoctrinated, having surely paid my dues. From that day forward I embraced the Bills as a part of my soul, never suspecting the pain this would bring me, nor that there would be no turning back. I would shed tears over the Bills. I would even spill some blood.

The freakish torment endured by Buffalo Bills fans is undisputed even by standards established among Boston Red Sox fans. Tell someone from almost anywhere in the world that you are a Bills fan—they'll wince or nervously laugh. They'll remind you of Scott Norwood, of the four straight Super Bowl losses. Bills fans will remind them of the four straight AFC championships, and the greatest comeback in NFL history. They might quip: "O.J. couldn't have been guilty. The Bills don't stab—they choke!" Some Bills fans might respond by choking *them*.

But the essence of being a Bills fan, for me, goes much further than any Scott Norwood field goal attempt or last-ditch Tennessee Titan lateral could ever travel, regardless of how wide right or suspiciously forward it might be.

Because when I think about the Bills and why it is that I intertwine myself with them so deeply, I always return to my favorite memories, back to the days when I was 12 years old, thumbing it out to the stadium with my buddies, sneaking into games, sitting wherever we wanted because we knew all the ushers.

Unexpectedly, in 1980, out of the red, white and blue, the Bills, perennial worst team in the league, had the colossal gall to actually be good. Few people outside Buffalo would ever remember this '80 team and many younger Bills fans just can't relate. Somehow, sandwiched between all the old AFL glory of the 1960s, the futility of the 1970s, and the Super Bowl runs of the early 1990s, a brief but magical chapter in Bills history got lost.

It began on September 7, 1980. That day the Bills beat the Dolphins for the first time in a full decade, ending the longest losing streak against a single opponent in NFL history. The Bills, coached by Chuck Knox in his third year, opened the season 5–0. These Bills would go on to win the AFC East for the first time since the division was created in the 1970 AFL/NFL merger. This was a hard-earned division crown. During the regular season the Bills beat all of the NFL's elite, including both the Pittsburgh Steelers and the Los Angeles Rams, combatants in the prior season's Super Bowl (played in January 1980) as well as the Oakland Raiders, who would go on to win the 1980 season's Super Bowl. All of this came 14 years removed from the last meaningful Bills campaign, when they won the AFL's Eastern division but lost the AFL Championship game, missing out on a chance to play in the first Super Bowl in January 1967.

By sheer coincidence, the fall of 1980 saw a civic pride movement spearheaded by the Buffalo Chamber of Commerce take off just as the Bills' fortunes did. The centerpiece of the media campaign was a television commercial that ran on all the local stations. It featured an energetic brunette woman in a red blazer who had a gravity-defying stride leading a parade of beaming blue-collar types around town, all of them singing a snappy song, "Buffalo's got a spirit, talking proud, talking proud . . ."

Late in that season the "Talking Proud" tune was played at a few home games after touchdowns and at the end of victorious contests. Once, after an overtime victory against the Rams, the players came back on the field, some half dressed, just to dance around as the fans romped in the stands. The 30-second song, something more akin to a corny supermarket jingle you'd hear on AM radio than to a sports anthem, somehow captured the city's heart and became this infectious battle cry that carried over into the next season. And then, just like that, the Talking Proud campaign quietly disappeared, save for the few scattered street signs around town that to this day still have the red and white charging Buffalo logo etched on them.

This 1980 Bills team, led on offense by quarterback Joe Ferguson, running back Joe Cribbs, and wide receivers Jerry Butler and Frank Lewis, and on defense by the Bermuda Triangle of Fred Smerlas, Shane Nelson and Jim Haslett, has been unfairly discarded in the annals of football lore. No, these Bills didn't reach the Super Bowl; they didn't even win their playoff game. But they had guts and heart and many memorable characters, such as Conrad Dobler, a.k.a. "the dirtiest player in football," and Phil Villapiano, a star linebacker with the Raiders who when traded to Buffalo to play as a backup made the most of the humbling situation by becoming a valuable emotional leader. Smerlas and Haslett were the younger counterparts to vets Villapiano and Dobler, fast friends who ruled like savages on the field and who lived with equal ferocity off.

On January 3, 1981, the magical season came to an end with a heartbreaking playoff loss to the Chargers in San Diego. Forget wide right. The pain I felt as a Bills fan that day hurt worse than anything I'd ever feel as a result of the four straight Super Bowl defeats. The stakes were higher for this husky seventh-grader who'd hitched his hopes to the exciting bandwagon that rambled down Abbott Road just beyond my backyard.

These days, with the Drew Bledsoe era having unraveled and a new J.P. Losman chapter beginning, I find myself nostalgic not for Jim Kelly, Thurman Thomas or Andre Reed, but rather for Ferguson, Cribbs and Lewis. Memories come in a torrent of forgotten glory. Not all these memories are pleasant, but I'll take them. This was a great time to be a kid, and a Bills fan.

—July 25, 2005

CHAPTER ONE

THE STREAK IS OVER

People can talk all they want about the cold, snowy weather in Western New York, but I will tell you this much: On opening day at Rich Stadium, September 7, 1980, the sun was shining about as brilliantly as it ever has in Buffalo. And just like the saying goes, even a dog's ass gets a little sunshine every once in a while.

Buffalo played host to their archrivals, the Miami Dolphins. Only this wasn't so much a rivalry as it was an enslavement. The Dolphins had defeated the Bills a staggering 20 times in a row which remains to this day an NFL record.

Coming into that game, the Bills had not beaten the Dolphins since November of 1969. In the ensuing decade of the 1970s, Buffalo would never once beat the Dolphins. Although, why would they? The Dolphins were a great team; the Bills stunk. As a city we'd learned to accept it.

That morning, gambler/prognosticator-turned-CBS-television-personality Jimmy "the Greek" Snyder had the Bills as 3-point underdogs. "This game won't be any different than the past 20," he wrote in his column in the Sunday *Courier-Express*.

The Bills were coming off their fourth straight losing season. Their 1979 season mark of 7–9 would have been unacceptable by today's standards, but it was appreciated at the time by victory-starved Bills fans, who had, besides O.J. Simpson's rushing feats, little else to cheer about during the 1970s.

Neither did Buffalo. Between the sputtering steel plants, Bethlehem and Republic, double-digit unemployment levels overall, a decaying downtown, back-to-back disastrous ice and snow storms, not to mention the toxic Love Canal incident in nearby Niagara Falls, New York, it wouldn't have been unexpected for area residents to be in a collective state of woe heading into the 1980s. But Buffalo wasn't that way at all.

Most Buffalonians loved the region; couldn't imagine living anywhere else: generally clean, spacious environs, an abundance of salt-of-the-earth, good-humored people, affordable housing, quality hospitals, high schools and colleges, plenty of decent restaurants, music and nightlife. The Buffalo area survived just fine in spite of tough economic conditions and the insultingly long winters. If you did have a job (with Jimmy Griffin as mayor much of South Buffalo worked full-time for the city's police, fire, sanitation and parks departments), living costs were low, and besides, Buffalo had the Sabres, who fared well on the ice during the 1970s in the time of the French Connection, making it to but losing the 1975 Stanley Cup finals. Furthermore, there was easy access to Canadian beer just over the Peace Bridge. And of course, chicken wings.

The Bills, however, were at, or rather *were* the core of the Buffalo way of life. No matter how many times they made fans want to vomit, we kept coming back for more. The team wove Western New York together, and simultaneously tied us all into the fabric of the rest of the country in an exciting way, something vaguely tangible, something everyone could grab a slice of each Sunday, humiliating as it often was.

Even those seemingly indifferent, self-protectionist Bills fans who didn't see a need to read every word of coverage, in both papers, twice, or who didn't find it necessary to strategically turn between channels 2 and 7 to leverage every Rick Azar and Ed Kilgore sports segment, each day, yes even those fans often couldn't help themselves on Sundays. In those few remaining minutes before the clock struck 1 P.M. suddenly hope would live. Normally by 2 P.M. it would die.

But something, *something, I tell you,* was in the air that opening day. Some 80,020 fans—the first sell-out at Rich Stadium in five years, though not in time to lift the local television embargo—were on hand to greet the improved but still unpredictable Bills. Wearing white helmets, white jerseys and blue pants, the team took the field led by grim-faced coach Chuck Knox, in his third season. At quarterback was 30-year-old Joe Ferguson, No. 12.

Tough-as-nails with a stoic, rugged squint like Evel Knievel's, Ferguson would be flanked by one of the most talented receiving tandems the Bills had ever lined up—second-year speed merchant Jerry Butler and the sure-handed veteran Frank Lewis, rescued from oblivion by Knox a few seasons earlier as a castaway from the receiver-flush Pittsburgh Steelers.

Butler was coming off a phenomenal rookie season, as were three other promising second-year defensive players: nose tackle Fred Smerlas; linebacker Jim Haslett and free safety Jeff Nixon. Butler, Smerlas and Haslett were all named to the 1979 All-Rookie team. Haslett was named Defensive Rookie of the Year; Butler was named the all-around Rookie of the Year.

While the Bills were on the rise the Dolphins appeared to be fading. These fish were eight years removed from the perfect season in 1972. Venerated Dolphins coach Don Shula, at age 50 among the highest paid head coaches in pro football, was in tense contract negotiations with owner Joe Robbie and the Miami front office during the weeks leading up to the opener. Despite rumors he was flirting with Notre Dame, Shula inked a fresh four-year deal just two days before the game, providing a gust of morale for the Dolphins coming into Orchard Park.

Apart from a few veterans, such as quarterback Bob Griese and All-Pro lineman Bob Kuechenberg (who once told a reporter "Buffalo will never beat Miami as long as I'm playing"), the Dolphins comprised mostly young unknowns; half of their 45-man roster were players in the league three years or less. Gone was the human steamroller Larry Csonka, who in 1979 had returned to Miami for one last season after spending a few years with the New York Giants. Csonka's replacement: a second-year blocking back out of Baylor, the human push broom Steve Howell.

The Bills had lost to the Dolphins in every conceivable way during the streak—in blowouts, shutouts, squeakers, ref screwings, before small crowds, even one time on a nationally televised *Monday Night Football* season opener.

It was a uniquely impenetrable jinx. Just one year before, in the 1979 home opener, the Bills blew a chance to end the Dolphins curse in a driving rainstorm when Tom Dempsey missed a 34-yard field goal attempt in the closing seconds. Several years earlier, Dempsey, using all of half a foot encased in a specially made shoe, managed to set the record for longest field goal in the history of the NFL, and yet, when called upon for a chip shot by a Bills team down 9–7 to Miami, couldn't be bothered. Of course, it didn't help that the Bills were held to 5 first downs that day.

The 1980 opener against the Dolphins started out typically enough; the Bills were playing terribly. I listened to this game at full-blast on our big, wide, rectangular living room stereo, by myself, sporadically running outside in bursts of tantrum every time the Bills botched another series. It was classic Bills agony. On the opening kickoff, the usually ultra-conservative Chuck Knox surprisingly called for an onside kick. It failed. While the defense played solidly (Miami would be held to just 200 total yards), on offense the Bills simply could not score a touchdown. At times it felt like they would never, ever, score a touchdown.

Each time the Bills got something going they either fumbled or Ferguson threw an interception. Literally. Ferguson threw five picks that day, and he fumbled deep in Dolphin territory, as did fullback Curtis Brown. Rookie punter Greg Cater had one blocked in the third quarter and it set up a Miami touchdown, a 4-yard toss to Tony Nathan coming out of the backfield.

Here we go again, Ferguson thought to himself on the sidelines as Miami kicked the extra point.

Well into the fourth quarter the Bills still trailed 7–3, their lone score, a 40-yard second quarter field goal, set up by one of Jeff Nixon's diving interceptions. The Bills kicker that day was an ex-Falcon, Nick Mike-Mayer, he of the rare compound male surname which was pronounced "Mick-eh-meyer," though around Buffalo that morphed into "Kickameyer."

Even still, despite the numerous turnovers, the Bills defense kept the game close with a slew of their own takeaways—Nixon alone had three interceptions and a fumble recovery, seemingly always with Miami threatening—and Ferguson, despite the five interceptions, the sporadic boos, and his own fleeting gut feeling that the streak might never be broken, somehow refused to get down on himself.

Stranger yet, the fans seemed to have a mass hunch that victory was possible, no matter how jinxed the Bills had been against the despised Dolphins during an entire decade, and all afternoon.

With 6:44 left in the game, the Bills had the ball on their own 32. They trailed 7–3. Ferguson, snapping on his chin strap and jogging on the field to a smattering of boos overtaken by a howl of encouragement, knew it was now or never. He felt calm, and planned to utilize all the weapons at his disposal.

First, he grabbed some quick momentum with a 14-yard pass to Frank Lewis for a first down. On the next play, Ferguson slung a 9-yard pass to the versatile rookie Joe Cribbs out of the backfield, setting up another first down just inside Dolphin territory.

Then, in the single most pivotal play of the ballgame, Ferguson exploited free safety Glenn Blackwood, who was playing in deep zone coverage. With plenty of time, Fergy hit receiver Jerry Butler on a perfectly executed 29-yard down and out. The Bills had the ball first and ten on the Miami 11-yard line.

The mere proximity of the end zone stunned the 80,000 screaming fans. The opponent's goal line, a strange and distant place kept secretly hidden from the Bills offense for what seemed like a lifetime, was suddenly *11 yards away*. The *lead*—late in the fourth quarter—was in spitting distance. Against all that is rational, in the face of a most painfully certain outcome, the crowd sensed that something out of the ordinary was about to happen and just erupted.

And then, a whistle, offsides on the Dolphins—first and goal! Mayhem, panic—*oh, God, they're going to fumble*—excited disbelief—*please God*. On first down running back Curtis Brown pinched out two more yards, closer, closer, *were the Bills really going to score an actual touchdown*?

It was just me and WBEN radio's Van Miller at this point. Miller had an occasionally cruel and unusual play-by-play habit which left listeners twisting with each reinterpretation of what he thought he was seeing, sometimes rescinding basic calls, turning receptions into interceptions and then incompletions, well after you have already begun celebrating.

On second and goal, Ferguson rolled left and tossed a scary pass toward the left front corner of the end zone. A lone Dolphin lineman charging toward Ferguson leapt and swatted at the ball, but it sailed right through his arms, almost miraculously. The ball continued toward Ferguson's target, newly acquired backup fullback Roosevelt Leaks, who was straddled between two Dolphins, linebacker Rusty Chambers and free safety Tim Foley. Somehow the pass sliced through both sets of their marauding paws.

Miller made a gasping call that left no room for doubt:

"Ferguson rolling out. Looking. He throws toward the end zone . . . and it is CAUGHT for the touchdown! *Caught by Roosevelt Leaks!*"

Big Rosie Leaks, the ex-Colt, the rumbling, broad-shouldered fullback had, with 3:42 remaining, caught the ball two steps from the goal line and, losing his balance, lunged sideways with a crash into the end zone. The Bills offense raced to congratulate Leaks, Ferguson arriving last. From the end zone seats, a lone, lager-swilling zany known to his section simply as "The Goon," ran on to the field to join in the celebration and got close enough to pat Fergy on the helmet just as security converged on him.

The Bills now led 10–7. But *could* they hold? What legitimate reason was there to think *this* was really going to happen, that the Bills were going to beat the Dolphins? Of course they would blow it.

After the ensuing kickoff, Shula gave Griese the hook and inserted his backup, the younger, stronger-armed Don Strock. Over the years, no matter what the circumstance, Strock always seemed to come off the bench and pick apart the Bills secondary with playful indifference. When Strock appeared, my father would say, "This guy has our number." So, when Strock came in the game I took it as a foreboding development.

Griese isn't even hurt! Aw come on, not this guy!

Then, unbelievably, on third down, Strock tossed an interception! It was Bills linebacker Isiah "Butch" Robertson, the ex-Ram, one of several Knox veteran imports, who snared the ball around midfield. As Rich Stadium exploded wildly all around him, Robertson bounced and pranced all the way back down to the Dolphins 11. In a burst of exultation Robertson hurled the ball into the stands where a fan from Akron caught it.

Three plays later, on fourth down and inches at the 2, Cribbs went straight up and over the top for the victory-sealing touchdown. The extra point made it 17–7, Bills. The unfathomable was about to become reality. The Bills were going to beat the Dolphins.

Almost as impossibly, The Goon (who'd escaped the clutches of security guards in the end zone after the Leaks touchdown only later to be escorted from the stadium by reinforcements waiting for him in his section) had somehow managed to make it back to his seat again for the final gun.

In my living room Van Miller counted down the clock with a spontaneous mix of delight and reverence. "3-2-1 . . . the streak is over! Long live the streak . . ."

My 22-year-old brother Danny, who worked the game as an usher, to this day insists that it was the greatest moment in Bills history. Tens of thousands from the crowd stormed the field in a euphoric frenzy.

Here was a regular season game, a Week 1 opening game, and goal posts were being ripped down. Fans clawed up chunks of the turf as keepsakes and swarmed the players, who had launched into their own midfield victory celebration. A few fans somehow lifted the gargantuan veteran guard Reggie McKenzie off the ground. Linebackers Isiah Robertson and Jim Haslett lifted Coach Knox up on their shoulders under the blazing late afternoon sun. The tumult on the field, goalposts being paraded around the torn-up turf, fans drinking up the long-awaited moment of glory and final swills of Genesee backwash, lasted almost an hour. Many of the players came back out of the dressing room to marvel at the jubilant scene.

"This is my kind of town," laughed linebacker Phil Villapiano, as a fan patted him on the back and handed him a warm, half-empty can of Genny. Back in the locker room the longest-tenured Bill, McKenzie, who'd lost to the Dolphins more than any other man on earth, shouted, "We did it! We damn well did it!"

Owner Ralph Wilson later called it the greatest victory in the 20-year history of the Bills.

My brother Danny came home that day with a strange souvenir, a wooden Gatorade cup rack, apparently a staple of sideline necessities back then. It was blue and looked like the side of a *Buffalo Evening News* paperboy's wagon that had been riddled with tennis ball-sized holes. This strange object remained in the garage of our home on Tudor Boulevard for years to come, a constant reminder of that momentous day, a bizarre relic for the treasuring. It faded and cracked and got shuffled around different corners and nooks, but no one ever threw it out.

Bills fans went crazy for the simple reason that there hadn't really been anything to celebrate since December 18, 1966, when Jack Kemp led the Bills to a win at War Memorial Stadium against the Denver Broncos to claim their third straight AFL East title, a generation ago, before the merger of the AFL and NFL, before they even had Super Bowls. The goal posts came down that day too. Two weeks later, on New Year's Day of 1967, in Buffalo, the Bills lost the AFL Championship game to the Kansas City Chiefs in a rout, 31–7, missing out on a chance to play in—and most likely lose—the first-ever Super Bowl to Vince Lombardi's Green Bay Packers.

For longsuffering Bills fans, perhaps in the way a deathly parched shipwreck survivor is overcome by delirium, ending the streak *felt* like winning the Super Bowl. Finally beating the Dolphins cast an astonishing buzz over the entire city. That night Bob Seger played the last of three sold-out shows at Memorial Auditorium. At one point, he announced proudly to the crowd that he'd been at the game, driving the fans wild. I'd like to think he credited the Bills for finally beating the Dolphins after all these years and then broke into a heartfelt rendition of "Against the Wind," but I'm sure he probably performed some other new song while he had the crowd on his side. It is said that Allentown, home to Mulligan's Brick Bar and its alter-ego, The Pink Flamingo, rocked that night like never before, as revelers soaked up more beer and a truly wonderful moment in time. Down on Seneca Street, the legendary nightspot The Pierce Arrow was jammed, and many of the Bills players showed up after the game to carry the celebration long into the magnificent Indian summer night.

As a seventh-grader still a year or so away from my first beer, I celebrated in my own way. I remember momentarily thinking that perhaps school would be closed the following day, quickly realizing that was a silly thought. I remember lingering in my driveway. I could have just as easily sat on the front porch, but for some reason I chose to stand in my driveway, surveying my neighborhood just a few miles from the stadium, listening to faraway cheers, honking horns, distant shrieks, watching my smiling neighbors and waiting for the Gallivan brothers to come over and relive the whole thing.

"I thought for sure we were going to lose," I told John

Gallivan. He did too. That evening all the kids on Tudor played football in the street until our legs fell off.

History, with the benefit of hindsight, will often retroactively assign certain events the distinction of being turning points, but in this case there was no mistaking it. A new Bills era had officially begun.

CHAPTER TWO

SETTING THE STAGE

Bills fans had no idea what lay ahead following the mayhem of opening day, although clearly the foundation for a winning season had been established. At least one Bill suspected back in training camp that a potentially special year loomed ahead.

A few weeks into camp, which was being held that unusually muggy summer for the 14th and final time at Niagara University, All-Pro linebacker Phil Villapiano, recently traded to the Bills from the Oakland Raiders, was sitting around the Clet Hall cafeteria, a short jog from Alumni Field. It was between morning and afternoon practice sessions and a few veterans, among them Reggie McKenzie, had just finished lunch.

Villapiano, a bushy-haired, wide-smiling veteran acquired by Chuck Knox in exchange for Bills wide receiver Bobby Chandler, had become a popular character around camp. Out of left field Villapiano asked McKenzie, "Hey Reggie, why don't you guys ever win up here?"

McKenzie was by far the baddest-ass Bill there was, period. Part of the fabled Electric Company offensive line that blocked O.J. Simpson to his record-breaking

2003-yard-season in 1973, McKenzie was one of only a handful of players left from the Simpson era which had ended at the culmination of the 1977 season with The Juice being traded to the San Francisco 49ers. No one, not fellow players, not coaches, not reporters, nobody ever dared trifle with McKenzie. He was a doorframe-filling enormity who with his Isaac Hayes gold chain and aviator sunglasses projected an almost mythical coolness wherever he strode. Only his Bills ball cap made him seem remotely human.

When Villapiano asked that question, McKenzie glared at the ex-Raider as if he'd just insulted his mother.

"Why don't we win?"

"Yeah *win*," Villapiano reiterated. "Why don't you guys ever seem to win up here?"

Before McKenzie could articulate even a cursory response (most fans blamed Ralph Wilson, probably unfairly, for failing to invest in a defense to complement The Juice) or, alternatively, rip Villapiano's head off, the new veteran wisely steered their conversation in a positive direction.

"Because, you know, from what I've seen so far in camp there are a helluva lot of great players on this ball club," Villapiano explained.

Indeed, just competing for the 31-year-old Villapiano's position was a brigade of talented linebackers: wild child Jim Haslett, in his second year; speedy Lucius Sanford, in his third year; Shane Nelson, who hit like a jackhammer, in his fourth; not to mention ex-Ram All-Pro Isiah Robertson. Everywhere he looked he saw quality players. Villapiano was amazed he had never even heard of 6'6" offensive tackle Joe Devlin, anonymous around the league playing alongside McKenzie and five-time Pro Bowler Joe DeLamielleure, and yet here was an ox-strong warrior who looked to be on the verge of a dominating year. Undrafted free agent guard Tim Vogler was equally impressive. Also surprising to Villapiano was the sharp passing game. Who knew Joe Ferguson, for so many years viewed as a mere conduit between center Mike Montler and O.J. Simpson, could throw the football with such velocity and uncanny precision? The Bills receivers, 23-year-old deep threat Jerry Butler and cagey possession man Frank Lewis, ten years Butler's senior, seemed to perfectly complement one another. Then there was the rookie, Joe Cribbs, the little halfback from Auburn who was turning heads with his pass catching abilities coming out of the backfield.

"I mean you got great players here Reggie!" Villapiano explained. "A lot more talent than the Raiders ever had, and the Raiders are good! I'm telling you, we just need to get these young guys believing in themselves."

Among the early believers in the possibility that success was at hand was Coach Knox. He'd patiently rebuilt the team with a mix of youth and experience, speed and toughness. Knox wanted the Bills to be the Raiders of the East, assembling animals, speed freaks, brawlers, crazies—guys who would go out and literally *beat the shit* out of the opponent each Sunday. Knox didn't care much what they did off the field. But he had vowed to Ralph Wilson that he would get the Bills to the playoffs.

"The fans in Buffalo are the most loyal in the country," Wilson told Knox during one of their first sit-down meetings back in early January of 1978 following the miserable '77 season. The Bills owner had made a special recruiting trip to Knox's home in Southern California to personally pitch him on the job.

Wilson knew the fans deserved more than 3–11, and to some extent understood why he had become the target of their frustration. Beloved today, Wilson in the late 1970s was viewed by some in Buffalo as a skinflint, and worse, a highfalutin aristocrat who bred horses and played tennis. Primarily responsible for Wilson's "outsider" status was the not so subtle fact that he maintained his residence in Michigan, in the exclusive Detroit suburb of Grosse Pointe Shores.

What fans didn't realize was how determined Wilson had been to bring winning football to Buffalo. That the dashing millionaire from Detroit even bought and placed a football team in Western New York at all was a complete fluke. As part of the eight-member "Fool's Club" in 1959 hell-bent on creating a brand new American Football League to rival the National Football League, Wilson originally wanted to put his franchise in Miami. He owned a winter home there, and better yet, the Orange Bowl was one of the best stadiums in the country. Wilson, a trucking/insurance magnate with a small piece of the NFL Detroit Lions, thought he had an easy sell. But Miami luminaries—politicians, sportswriters, and especially the University of Miami football people—were all opposed to his plans.

A decade earlier, the sunny beach community had tried and failed, spectacularly as it turned out, to launch a team, the Miami Seahawks, part of the short-lived All-America Football Conference that existed between 1946 and 1949. After that experience, Miami wanted no part of the AFL, seen by city leaders as a newfangled, equally doomed version of the AAFC. Miami's Seahawks had drawn so few spectators, the franchise nearly bank-rupted the upstart league before it even got off the ground. The Seahawks of South Florida lasted all of one year before migrating to Baltimore, becoming the Colts in 1947.

Buffalo had an AAFC team too. Call them the first it-eration of the Bills. But unlike Miami, the franchise was greatly appreciated. Just like the AFL, the AAFC was launched as a rival to the NFL. It first took shape a few days before D-Day in 1944 with a meeting in St. Louis organized by Chicago newspaperman Arch Ward, cred-ited for thinking up baseball's all-star game. Ward in-vited a group of investors that included sports figures such as boxer Gene "Long Count" Tunney and Holly-wood movie star Don Ameche. The league started play in September 1946 with eight teams: the Brooklyn Dodgers, Buffalo Bisons, Chicago Rockets, Cleveland Browns, Los Angeles Dons, Miami Seahawks, New York Yankees and San Francisco 49ers. Hardly even a histori-cal footnote today, the AAFC began its life with lots of promise—the end of World War II offered a bumper crop of young talent coming back home—and plenty of hype, mainly centered around Paul Brown's Cleveland Browns, an instant powerhouse considered as good, if not better, than any NFL team.

Buffalo's team was owned by a pair of local oilmen, Jim Breuil and Ray Ryan, who called their franchise the Bisons after the old Buffalo Bisons football teams that were part of the original NFL in the roaring '20s. Those Bisons were, in turn, offshoots of the former Buffalo All Americans from the long-defunct American Professional Football Association, forerunner to the NFL. The APFA came about in the late summer of 1920, hatched in an auto showroom in Canton, Ohio. The All Americans, who joined this new league alongside teams like the Canton Bulldogs, Muncie Flyers and Columbus Panhandles, historically consisted of the best players from the various semi-pro teams in and around Buffalo, company-sponsored squads whose origins went all the way back to the earliest part of the 20th century and whose names included the "South Parks," "Niagaras," and the "Pierce Arrows," named for the popular automobile manufactured by George Pierce, the Henry Ford of Buffalo.

Possibly the first instance of a Buffalo football screwing came in 1921, during the second year of the APFA. The All Americans had cruised through the season as the fledgling league's only unbeaten team. But in the final game of the season, December 4, 1921, they lost to the Chicago Staleys. Both teams finished with nine victories. Just one week earlier, on Thanksgiving Day, Buffalo had beaten Chicago, 7–6. But Chicago's star player-coach George Halas argued that the rematch had effectively constituted the championship, even though Buffalo insisted there should have been one more game for all the marbles. The league owners sided with Halas, and the title went to Chicago.

The following year, the American Professional Football Association changed its name to the National Football League; the Buffalo All Americans finished near the bottom. In 1924, the All Americans became the Bisons, but by 1929, as the early stages of the Great Depression began to roil Western New York, the Bisons folded.

Although Buffalonians were thrilled in 1946 to see the Buffalo Bisons reincarnated as part of the new AAFC, management decided they wanted a new name to differentiate the team from the city's minor league baseball and hockey teams. So Breuil, owner of the Frontier Oil Company, held an off-season contest to rename the team. Since the oil company was starting a new "frontier" in Western New York sports history, one creative entrant suggested that the football team should be named after fabled Western frontiersman Buffalo Bill Cody. William Frederick Cody, incidentally, was given his nickname by railroad workers a few years after the end of the Civil War. Cody, a celebrated Cavalry scout and a one-time Pony Express rider, had been hired by the Kansas Pacific Railroad to hunt buffalos full-time, providing the primary source of food for the track layers. Cody and his rifle dispatched the woolly creatures with such proficiency that the laborers, who choked down buffalo meat morning, noon and night, and who were always surrounded by piles of bones and carcasses, slapped Cody with his famous nickname which at the time already belonged to an equally skilled buffalo hunter, Buffalo Bill Comstock. In 1947, Breuil adopted the nickname for his football team.

One season later, in 1948, the Buffalo Bills played in the AAFC title game against those mighty Cleveland Browns, featuring such hallowed players as Otto Graham and Lou Groza. The Bills were dismantled, 49–7. The Browns would go on to win all four AAFC titles.

When the AAFC passed away in'49, the notion of true professional football in Buffalo expired along with it. For four years Buffalo fans had packed Civic Stadium on Jefferson Avenue and Best Street on Buffalo's heavily German and Polish East Side. Fans waited in line for hours around Christmas of 1949 to buy season tickets when there had been excited talk that the three most successful AAFC franchises, Cleveland, San Francisco and Buffalo, would be folded into the NFL. But it never panned out. The NFL selected Cleveland, San Francisco and, to the surprise of many people around the sport, *Baltimore*.

Turns out that George Preston Marshall, then the owner of the NFL's Washington Redskins, had argued that the lowly Baltimore franchise, while not particularly impressive either on the field or at the box office, would serve as a nice rivalry for his Skins, and fellow owners went along with his rationale. (This is the same George Preston Marshall who came up with the idea of moving the goal posts from the back of the end zone up to the goal line.)

The Bills, with a furious ground attack led by Harry Hopp and Chet Mutryn, were the only team not to lose to the Browns in 1949 (tying them twice), and even though attendance at Civic Stadium was among the best in the league, Buffalo was passed over by the NFL. That first NFL Baltimore Colts team was so miserably sub par it was shut down after only one season. But it was too late. There would be no football in Buffalo for a full decade. Baltimore would be awarded a second franchise in 1953. By that time, many of the old Bills had signed on with the Browns. Civic Stadium became a venue for stock car racing during the 1950s. Then came Ralph Wilson to the rescue.

In October of 1959, Wilson, spurned by Miami, met with some Buffalo people, among them Paul Neville, sports editor of *The Buffalo Evening News*, who urged him to put his new NFL franchise in Buffalo. The city, Neville pleaded, was ravenous for football. Wilson was sold. The new Bills would be part of the AFL when it made its debut in 1960 and would play in the newly re-named War Memorial Stadium, capacity 46,000.

Wilson loved that Buffalo was a football town. It reminded him of industrial Detroit. He told friends at cocktail parties that owning the AFL Bills was like owning a racehorse. "You just kind of assume you're not going to make any money but it's a fun thing to do," he'd say, pointing out "there was always a chance that your horse could win the Kentucky Derby."

But Wilson's high society friends laughed at him, privately and to his face. His buying into the AFL, in Buffalo no less, would be like today if someone purchased an Arena Football League franchise in Schenectady.

Skeptics had given the AFL maybe a year, at best two. But Wilson was more optimistic, and he loved football. Born in Columbus, Ohio, Wilson moved to Detroit as a kid and grew up going to all of the University of Detroit and NFL Lions home games with his insurance executive father, Ralph Wilson, Sr.

For the first three years in Buffalo, Wilson lost money on his new investment, but never thought about throwing in the towel. Attendance at War Memorial was growing—the Bills averaged crowds of 15,000 that first season of 1960; by the third season, average attendance was up to 25,000. That was because the Bills were getting better, notching five wins in their inaugural season in 1960, six wins in 1961 and seven in 1962. By 1963 the Bills finished at 7–6–1, tied for first in the AFL Eastern Division with the Boston Patriots, setting the stage for the first-ever modern Bills playoff game, December 28, 1963.

The Bills lost, 26–8, in a snowstorm at War Memorial Stadium.

But the Bills were on the brink of football nirvana. Featuring quarterbacks Jack Kemp and Daryle Lamonica, receiver Elbert Dubenion and running back Cookie Gilchrist, the Bills would go on to play in three straight AFL Championships, winning two of them. It seemed like quality football and Buffalo would become synonymous. But as the years passed the Bills drifted further and further into pro football's backwater.

Fed up, Wilson hired Chuck Knox on January 11, 1978. After years of heavy-handed involvement in football operations, Wilson divorced himself from the process and turned the reigns fully over to Knox. The Bills organization took Western New York by surprise when they announced that they'd signed the 46-year-old coach of the Los Angeles Rams to a six-year contract. Even Bills fans had to wonder why a proven winner like Knox would want to come to Buffalo from L.A.

My brother Shawn and I heard it on the car radio, on the way to hockey practice at the outdoor Cazenovia Park ice rink where my father drove the Zamboni part-time. Dad summarized the news for us: "The Bills got a good coach."

Indeed, at the time, the name Chuck Knox was up there in stature with known, respected, winning coaches, not exactly a name like Tom Landry or Chuck Noll (okay maybe Chuck Knox is a name like Chuck Noll, almost to the letter come to think of it), but if Knox wasn't A+ he certainly was A-list, up there with Raiders coach John Madden and Vikings coach Bud Grant. Knox had taken the Rams to *five* straight NFC West Division titles. During his five-year stay in L.A. between 1973 and 1977 the Rams lost only 15 regular season games.

Knox was a product of what is considered by many to be the cradle of football, Western Pennsylvania's Steel Valley. He was born Charles Robert Knox on April 27, 1932 in Sewickley, a desolate town on the Ohio River, built around mills, mines and foundries.

Chuck's childhood friends called him Nick, and he grew up slugging. His mother Helen, a Scottish immigrant, was a big, hard woman. She scrubbed floors for some of Sewickley's wealthy families. His father Charlie, an Irish immigrant, was a stocky steelworker with an ice box for a chest. Charlie Knox drove a beer truck evenings delivering suds to the town's gin mills and pool halls. He'd spend the second half of his evenings at those same taverns, swilling and brawling away the suffocating sense of desolation that permeates life in towns like Sewickley. Charlie Knox could be a mean drunk. He'd beat up Chuck and his brother Billy for even the slightest infractions or sometimes for no reason at all. If teenage Chuck had to go out to a bar to drag his father Charlie out of a scuffle, afterwards when they got home, his father would beat him up for breaking it up. Knox took after his father, always getting into scrapes with kids in his Walnut Street neighborhood. Charlie Knox used to tell his son, "Don't come home crying after getting a beating, or you'll get another beating."

When his father was laid off from the steel mill, Knox, then just 16, lied about his age to get a non-union job in a railroad yard making 83 cents an hour blowtorching old Pennsylvania Railroad cars into scrap metal. It was his first taste of a possible future, one he was determined to avoid.

Chuck Knox excelled in football, which, besides molten steel, was the essence of Western Pennsylvania.

He starred as an offensive guard and linebacker for Quaker Valley High. Knox's style was to intimidate, to hit harder than anyone on the field. In drills teammates tried to avoid him. But so did college scouts, even though he was a reputable senior linebacker in football's hotbed. Finally, a scout for tiny Juniata College in central Pennsylvania named Tommy "Midget" Perricelli came to see Knox play. After the game, in the locker room, Knox grabbed the scout and shook him, yelling, "If you just come back for me you'll get a great player!"

Perricelli did, and over the objections of his old man, Chuck Knox left town in August 1950 for the three-hour drive to Juniata in Huntingdon, Pa. Tucked away in the Allegheny Mountains, Juniata had a small but well-run football program. Knox played offensive tackle. But after a freshman year spent boozing, getting into fights and chasing skirts, Knox was in danger of flunking out. A summer back home in the steel mills wisened him up. By the start of his sophomore year Knox decided to hit the books.

On the field, Knox was hitting everything in sight. He was always getting into fights, often drawing late hit penalties, so many in fact that he was once benched. But Knox was a natural leader, serving as co-captain his senior year when Juniata had its first-ever undefeated season.

Knox was honest enough with himself to know he'd never make it to the NFL, not as a player anyway. But he could perhaps make it as a coach. After graduating with a degree in history in 1954, Knox soon realized football coaching jobs were a scarcity. Married to his wife Shirley while still in college and by now a young father himself, Knox took an unpaid job as an assistant at his alma mater, working for his old coach Bob Hicks. He later became a low-paid high school coach in Elwood City, a 15,000-person mill town 30 miles north of Pittsburgh that he knew quite well while growing up. The smallest high school in its athletic division, Elwood City was always getting pounded by bigger, stronger teams, such as Butler or the squad from Beaver Falls, which featured a brilliant quarterback named Joe Namath. But Knox loved the underdog element of coaching Elwood City, and saw to it that his players embraced this "we'll show them" spirit. But toiling away as a high school coach in a town surrounded by smokestacks was not exactly his dream job.

In March of 1959, Knox's prayers were answered when he got a call from Paul Amen, the head coach at Wake Forest. Amen wanted an assistant coach to increase the Demon Deacons' scouting presence in Western Pennsylvania. Knox got the job, later became offensive line coach and a few years after that moved on to an assistant coaching position with the University of Kentucky. *That* was the big-time career boost Knox had needed.

The Wildcats brilliant head coach, Blanton Collier (who would later coach the Browns) had just lost an assistant and protégé, Don Shula, who was a former defensive back with the Browns and Colts. Shula had taken a defensive coordinator job with the Detroit Lions. Collier was not only looking to replace Shula, he'd been contemplating switching his offensive line coach, Bill Arnsparger, to defensive line. Knox, recommended to Collier by a Wildcat assistant named Bill Crutchfield, was hired as offensive line coach.

Knox didn't know it but he was about to get the break of his life and play a role in one of the most famous watershed moments in the history of pro football.

In 1963, the three-year-old AFL welcomed into its tent the newly renamed New York Jets. The franchise's forefather, the New York Titans, had gone broke, snatched up by a group of five high-net-worth individuals that included television executive Sonny Werblin and oilman Leon Hess. Not long after buying the team, Werblin announced that its colors were being changed from black and gold to green and white, and that he had just signed a new coach from the NFL by the name of Weeb Ewbank.

A short, quiet, crew-cutted mathematician of the game, Ewbank had coached offensive line for the AAFC Browns during their four-year lock on the ill-fated league. He later transformed the beleaguered Baltimore Colts franchise, coaching them to victory in the monumental 1958 title game against the New York Giants that put football on the American map at the dawn of television. But despite leading the Colts to two championships, Ewbank was placed on a short leash. Baltimore's owner, a local businessman named Carroll Rosenbloom, fired him after the 1962 season. To replace Ewbank, Rosenbloom hired Don Shula, only 33 at the time.

Slapped in the face, Ewbank spent the summer of 1963 plotting his return to coaching glory. Setting up Jets headquarters at Peekskill Military Academy on the Hudson River, Ewbank began to assemble a coaching staff. Looking for the best young talent available, Ewbank snared Walt Michaels, a former Green Bay Packer linebacker who at the time was an assistant with the

Oakland Raiders. Michaels would coach defensive line. As his offensive line coach, Ewbank hired 31-year-old Chuck Knox.

Paid an annual salary of $11,000, Knox earned every penny when a few years later he helped lure Joe Namath to the Jets. Namath was a superstar coming out of Alabama but his NFL rights belonged to the St. Louis Cardinals. A bidding war over the talented quarterback had broken out, but Knox had the ace in the hole. He'd known Namath personally since the star quarterback was in the eighth grade. When Knox coached at tiny Elwood City High School, Namath played for rival Beaver Falls. Knox had recruited Namath's brother, Frank, to Kentucky, and had tried to make Joe Namath a Wildcat as well. With Chuck Knox there to hold his hand (and Werblin there to write a fat check) Namath signed with the Jets.

With Namath at quarterback, Ewbank took revenge on Rosenbloom and Shula on January 12, 1969, in Super Bowl III, where the Jets upset the Colts in a victory so famously guaranteed. But more profoundly, the Jets had furnished the AFL with instantaneous legitimacy. The two leagues officially merged a year later.

Three years after the Jets shocked the Colts, owner Carroll Rosenbloom shocked the football world when he traded his franchise, among the most successful in the history of the sport, to Chicago industrial tycoon Robert Irsay, who had just purchased the Los Angeles Rams for $19 million. Rosenbloom, a Baltimore native, moved to Los Angeles and took over the Rams. Under coach Tommy Prothro, the Rams finished 6–7–1 in 1972. Rosenbloom had his general manager Don Klosterman, brought along from Baltimore, summarily execute Prothro and his entire staff, and they soon began interviewing for head coaches. On their shortlist: Chuck Knox.

By this time Knox, like Shula, had moved through the Kentucky Wildcat pipeline to an assistant job with the Lions, making around $20,000 a year and a name for himself as another Blanton Collier-produced football genius. During an early meeting, Rosenbloom and Knox hit it off marvelously. Rosenbloom offered Knox $50,000 over three years and the 41-year-old promptly replied, "Where do I sign?"

His dream of becoming an NFL head coach had finally come true.

In his first season, Knox didn't disappoint. He led the Rams to a 12–2 record, and was named Coach of the Year. His Rams later lost to the Dallas Cowboys in the divisional playoff round, 27–16, and between 1974–76 the Rams lost three straight NFC Championship games. Then, in 1977, the Rams lost a first-round playoff game to the Vikings, 14–7, in the famous "Mud Bowl," a game played in such thick, dark slop that on television, against the backdrop of the night sky, the muck-laden players were barely visible to viewers.

After that loss, the Rams fanatical owner, obsessed with winning the Super Bowl, decided he'd had enough of Knox. Rosenbloom instructed his longtime GM Klosterman to start looking for a replacement for Knox, calling his style of play "too boring to watch." Knox, for his part, would later retort that "the only dull football is losing football."

Dull, perhaps, but Knox's brand was time-tested, fundamental football. "Ground Chuck," as the L.A. sportswriters dubbed him, had a propensity to establish a running game even if it killed him—or his owner. Incidentally, not long after shoving Knox out of L.A., Rosenbloom mysteriously drowned in heavy surf near Miami Beach.

Knox could have landed in Detroit where he had ties to the organization, or Kansas City, who would ultimately sign Marv Levy of the Canadian Football League, but always a fan of the underdog, Knox took on the challenging, potentially career-defining project of rebuilding the rockbottomed Buffalo Bills. Knox's six-year deal was worth around $200,000 per year. His hire came as something of a surprise to Bills fans long under the impression that a coach of Knox's caliber would never come to Buffalo. The local media seemed sure the Bills were going after former 49ers coach Monte Clark or Stanford University's Bill Walsh.

Knox's tough public persona belied a much friendlier demeanor on display in abundance behind the scenes. He was what football people call a "player's coach." That is, he wasn't a hardcore disciplinarian like a Don Shula or Tom Landry, who demanded order and accounted more to management. Knox, on the other hand, encouraged individuality, preferred wildness. One day, after a road game, Knox showed up at practice with a scrape across his nose and a trace of a black eye, and since it was no secret Knox liked to throw back a few whiskeys after a game, it didn't take long for his players to figure out that their coach had been in a barroom brawl.

"You should see the other three guys," Knox cracked, before any of the players could say a word to him.

No dress code for road trips, no fines for missing meetings. "Don't throw the ball so far over the fence you can't find it," he'd tell his players after games, knowing full well that most were going out partying.

Knox loved to mix it up—he'd line up in a three-point stance, his ball cap turned backwards, ready to butt heads with players in full equipment. His guys always knew where they stood with him.

"I hope I didn't waste a second-round pick on you," a disgusted Knox once told Fred Smerlas before practice early in the 1979 regular season, Smerlas's first as a Bill. "Big strong Greek? A real tough-ass, huh? Well, you ain't shit. You should be killing people and you aren't doing a goddamn thing!" Smerlas took it hard, thinking for a day or two he might be out of football soon enough. But, by the end of that year, Smerlas was angling for Mike Kadish's starting job—he literally demanded the job. When Knox told him "We'll see," Smerlas responded, "Fuck you, I want to start!" A slap-fight ensued. It's hard to imagine Tom Landry in a slap-fight with an obstinate rookie. Then again, Landry never coached Fred Smerlas.

Knox was taking over for one of the losingest coaches in Bills history, Jim Ringo. Ringo had been Lou Saban's offensive line coach. When Saban burned out midway through the 1976 season, it was on Ringo to pick up the pieces. As a player, Ringo went to seven straight Pro Bowls, an undersized but quick center around whom Vince Lombardi built his power sweep offense at the dawn of the Packer dynasty. As head coach of the Bills, Ringo would go 3–20 over one and two-third seasons, including an unholy stretch of 14 straight losses between 1976–77.

The bottom of the Ringo sinkhole came midway through the 1977 season in an ugly pounding at the hands of the expansion Seattle Seahawks, a road game in which O.J. Simpson blew out his knee.

Simpson attained superstardom playing in Buffalo but few wins. The Bills went 41–75 during the O.J. years (1969–1977), with one playoff appearance in 1974, a game the wildcard Bills lost to the Steelers, 32–14. During the decade of the 1970s, only two teams, the New Orleans Saints (42–98–4) and the New York Giants (50–93–1), would lose more regular season games than the Bills (51–91–2).

Knox, whose official title was vice president in charge of football operations, was determined to change all of that. He had control of all player moves, drafting, trading, scouting. He'd snickered privately when he first started that the Bills had run scouting "out of a shoebox."

In late January of 1978, Dallas had just beaten the Denver Broncos in the forgettable Super Bowl XII at the Superdome and Knox was assembling his coaching staff, enlisting many of his former Rams assistants, including defensive coordinator Tom Catlin, offensive coordinator Ray Prochaska, defensive backs coach Jim Wagstaff and quarterbacks coach Kay Stephenson. With full decision-making power, Knox readied for his first significant maneuver as coach of the Bills: O.J. Simpson was to be offloaded.

Knox met with Simpson on January 30th. Simpson still had one year left on his contract. Afterwards, Simpson publicly indicated he'd like to play out his last year in Buffalo, even though just a few years earlier Simpson made it no secret he wanted to be traded to a West Coast team to accommodate his increasingly burgeoning acting pursuits. Privately, The Juice told Knox he wanted out of Buffalo. Next on Knox's to-do list: see that Simpson got his wish.

On March 24th, Knox, along with Bills GM Bob

Lustig, pulled off what in hindsight has to be one of the best trades in football history, shipping 31-year-old Simpson to the San Francisco 49ers in exchange for five top-round draft picks. The transaction was neatly brokered and finalized with 49ers GM Joe Thomas in the United Airlines Red Carpet Room at the San Francisco Airport in not much more time than it would have taken Simpson to race through the terminal to the Hertz counter and rent himself a car.

I remember the chilly gray March evening when my older brother Danny broke the news that the Bills had traded O.J. Me and my brother Shawn were tossing a baseball on the front lawn after supper in the evening twilight of the early spring. Danny was talking to someone on the pea-green kitchen wall phone, but he was in the driveway, having achieved the privacy a stretch of the cord into the back hall and out the storm door provided. He shouted, "The Bills traded O.J.!" I couldn't comprehend it, and got terribly upset. "Why?! How could they?" I distinctly remember Danny saying later it didn't matter anyway because "his knees were shot." Danny didn't seem the least bit bothered, but I took the news hard. The Bills were one of the worst teams in the league, but at least we had O.J. Simpson, the greatest running back in the game. It was a source of tremendous pride that this national football hero played for our Buffalo Bills. Not anymore.

With O.J. gone it felt like there was no hope. Fergy could throw the ball downfield and accurately, but he had few quality targets. We had no speedy downfield threat. Our best wide receiver, Bobby Chandler, was either hurt or complaining or demanding to be traded. Tight end Reuben Gant often bungled passes earning him the nickname "Reuben Can't." There came a slew of new running backs, among them Terry Miller, a first round pick out of Oklahoma State in 1978, and fullback Curtis Brown. They were good players, but not The Juice.

Of course there was Simpson's perennial backup, Roland Hooks, who always showed flashes of superstar potential whenever given the chance. After Simpson blew out his knee in late October 1977, Hooks, a second-year player with 162 professional yards under his belt, started the next game against the New England Patriots. He promptly rushed for 155 yards, the best single-game rushing performance in the AFC that year. During an early season game against the Cincinnati Bengals in 1979, Hooks scored four touchdowns on four carries in a single half. He also once caught back-to-back Hail Mary's, including one for a touchdown, in the same last-ditch series against the Patriots. (That 1981 game at Rich Stadium was once considered the greatest Bills come-back, that is, before the Bills pulled off the single greatest comeback of all-time.) But for some reason Roland Hooks never started.

The O.J. trade was devastating to me, but in reality he was nearly out of football, and was more concerned with his Hollywood career at the time. In addition to the Hertz commercials, Simpson landed small roles in a few films, including "The Towering Inferno" and "Capricorn One," as well as the ABC landmark mini-series "Roots," which aired during the Blizzard of '77. Since school had been closed for two weeks on account of the storm, I was allowed to stay up late to watch "Roots" on TV, though I recall feeling hoodwinked a few nights into it realizing, around the time Ben Vereen's Chicken

George character started dominating the scenes, that O.J.'s African slave character would not be returning.

Simpson's ability to act was evidently sufficient enough to fool the 49ers organization into thinking his surgically repaired knee had fully healed. In his last year in Buffalo, Simpson earned $733,985, easily the highest annual salary in the NFL, and twice that of the next highest paid player, Joe Namath, who'd just finished out his career with the Rams. San Francisco picked up the last year of Simpson's contract and agreed to the shower of draft picks. That first season out of Buffalo, playing for the 49ers, Simpson gained 593 yards on 161 carries. In his final year in the NFL, Simpson, earning $806,668, would carry the ball just 120 times for 460 yards.

The Bills were owed: the 49ers' second and third round picks in the upcoming 1978 draft; the 49ers' first and fourth round picks in 1979 and one additional second-round pick in the 1980 draft.

Some of the picks would turn out to be busts. With the first two Simpson-linked draft choices, Knox took underwhelming defensive end Scott Hutchinson of Florida and the seldom-dangerous Danny Fulton, a wide receiver from football factory Nebraska-Omaha. But in the fourth round of the 1978 draft, Knox selected Georgia Tech linebacker Lucius Sanford, a second-team All-American.

Besides trading The Juice, perhaps the smartest move Knox made after arriving in Buffalo was a non-move. He stuck with Joe Ferguson at the quarterback position.

Even though Ferguson often struggled, faithful fans couldn't help but keep rooting for him. He just seemed like a good guy, and he could certainly play quarter-back. In 1976, Fergy set an NFL record when he tossed only one interception the entire season, albeit a season shortened by injury to seven games and 151 attempts. A year earlier, in 1975, while Simpson rushed for 1,817 yards and broke the record for touchdowns with 23, few remember Ferguson threw more touchdown passes (25) than any other quarterback in the league.

But when Fergy was having an off day, things could snowball. When he made a bad play, he sulked in his own self-deprecating manner, slowly walking back-ward, unhooking his chin strap, his head hung low, his hands on his hips. Often, he would clap his hands a few quick times as a way to stay upbeat. But when he was really playing lousy, he became rattled and useless. One of the things I remember about watching the Bills as a little kid was my father disappointingly identifying the exact moment when Ferguson's temper had done him in. "Aw, you see that," my dad would say, shaking his head. "There, he's down on himself. He's finished."

As much as people respected Ferguson's toughness, he was sometimes booed by the 30,000 or so fans that bothered to show up at Rich Stadium, among the league's most infrequently attended venues (unless of course the Rolling Stones were playing).

On opening day, 1978, Knox's first game as coach, the Bills hosted the Pittsburgh Steelers. By the end of the first half the Bills were losing 21-0. Ferguson was having a bad game, and the fans, more out of humorous drunken frustration than disdain for Fergy, began shouting, "We want Munson! We want Munson!" refer-ring to 37-year-old backup Bill Munson, picked up from San Diego that summer. Listening on the radio, I could hear the chants along with Van Miller's perplexed explanation. At the time it reminded me, a nun-fearing fifth-grader at St. Martin's School, of the story of the Crucifixion when the angry mob screamed "Give us Barabbus!" Munson, to the crowd's delight, eventually got in the game, as a result of Knox wanting to spare Ferguson the chance of being injured in a blowout, and the journeyman actually threw for a couple touchdowns. But the Bills still lost 28–17.

Munson would take a few more snaps late in the '78 season (including a two-interception second-half appearance in an embarrassing 31–10 loss to the inept Tampa Bay Bucs), but Knox always let Ferguson know he was the starter. His determination and leadership skills had won Knox over. The players respected Ferguson, and some were said to be afraid of him. In Week 5 of the 1978 campaign, Fergy had one of his best games ever, going 15 of 18, for 210 yards and two touchdown passes in a win over Marv Levy's Kansas City Chiefs. Fergy's 83 percent accuracy rate that afternoon is still a Bills record for highest one-game completion percentage.

But as improved as Ferguson was throwing the ball, the Bills finished 5–11 in Knox's first campaign. Embarrassingly, the Bills defense allowed 3,228 rushing yards in 1978, the most rushing yards allowed in one season—ever.

Still, there were some silver linings to be spotted in 1978 if one took the time to look. With only 18,084 season tickets sold that year, unfortunately not a lot of Buffalonians did. Highpoints included the thousand-yard season of rookie running back Terry Miller, who'd picked up 208 of them in a late November game against the New York Giants, joining O.J. Simpson and Cookie

Gilchrist in the annals of greatest rushing performances in franchise history. Also encouraging was the fact that the Bills lost seven of their games by no more than a touchdown. But most importantly, the Bills did not technically come in last place in the AFC East, as custom would have it. That's because on the final Sunday of the 1978 season—the NFL's first ever 16-game season—the Bills beat the Colts, 21–14 in Baltimore.

The win came on a fiercely windy day that saw Ferguson complete just three passes. The Bills could have just run for the bus as they had done so many times in prior seasons, but instead they played hard and won. It was Knox's first road win as Bills coach. And because both the Bills and the Colts finished 5–11, and because the Bills had beaten the Colts twice that year, the Bills appeared in the AFC East standings in fourth place.

Finally, out of the cellar, after going 2–14 in 1976 and 3–11 in 1977.

In early May of 1979, with the 49ers having finished the prior season with the worst record in the league (2–14), the Bills had the No. 1 pick overall. Knox, aided by his college scouting director Norm Pollom, chose little known but respected Ohio State linebacker Tom Cousineau.

Though he would eventually go on to spend four solid seasons with the Browns, Cousineau is among one of the more disappointing No. 1 picks of all-time. *Sports Illustrated* ran a feature story just after the Bills drafted Cousineau titled "You Made a Wise Choice." Cousineau, at the time the first Ohio State player ever to be picked No. 1 and only the second linebacker selected No. 1, had been presented as some sort of living, breathing spectacle of defensive prowess. Knox rated him the top athlete coming out of college that year, regardless of position. In his senior season of 1978, Cousineau set a record for tackles in one game (36 against Penn State), solo tackles in a season (244) and career tackles (647).

Everyone in town was thrilled to have the big Buckeye on the Bills. A native of suburban Cleveland, Cousineau was initially excited to hear he'd be going to Buffalo. But right at the gate it seemed the relationship was snakebitten. On the day of the draft, held then at the Waldorf-Astoria in midtown Manhattan, Cousineau shook hands with Pete Rozelle and went straight to the airport to fly to Buffalo for a press conference. At check-in, Cousineau was informed by the airline that there wasn't an available seat for his agent, Jimmy Walsh, who had famously represented Joe Namath. After the seating snafu was cleared up, and Cousineau and Walsh arrived in Buffalo, a dinner was scheduled with Stew Barber. Barber was a former offensive tackle on the AFL Bills championship teams who had recently been appointed as the Bills v.p. in charge of administration, which involved, among other things, handling all player signings.

Barber was instructed by Knox to play hardball with Cousineau. He'd made an initial offer that wasn't close to what Walsh envisioned for his client. Then Barber didn't show up for the dinner, and worse, he never even called the hotel to cancel. Furious, Jimmy Walsh made a hasty phone call to the Montreal Alouettes of the CFL. Walsh, incidentally, was part of a group that included Namath looking to buy the Alouettes at the time. By that evening, a deal had been struck: Cousineau was offered a three-year contract worth $850,000. Barber thought Walsh was bluffing. He'd offered $1.2 million for five years, a deal filled with performance clauses, and wouldn't budge. Cousineau signed with the Alouettes. He never played a down in Buffalo.

However, because the Bills had Cousineau's NFL rights, they were able to trade him to the Browns in 1982 for the pick that was ultimately used to draft Miami Hurricane quarterback Jim Kelly. In actuality, Kelly's first game in Orchard Park was in 1979 when Syracuse University, their new Carrier Dome under construction, "hosted" the Miami Hurricanes in a very special Rich Stadium edition of Orangemen football. The future Hall of Famer, then just a freshman, came off the bench in the third quarter and threw for a touchdown.

Despite the Cousineau debacle, Knox's drafting in 1979 was masterful. With nine picks in the top five rounds, Knox built himself a defense. He plucked two gems in the second round, Fred Smerlas, a defensive tackle from Boston College that Knox would transform into a nose guard to anchor his new 3–4 scheme, and Jim Haslett, a feisty linebacker from Indiana University of Pennsylvania. Haslett would soon make Bills fans forget all about Tom Cousineau.

That same year, in addition to the number one pick spent on Cousineau, the Bills were sitting on an additional first round pick—the fifth pick overall—used to snag Jerry Butler, a big-play receiver from Clemson where he set single-season and career receiving records despite a conservative offense. A native of Ware Shoals, South Carolina, Butler attended Clemson on a track scholarship. As a junior he won the Atlantic Coast Conference 60-yard dash.

Butler's blazing speed playing on the weak side would be the perfect complement to Frank Lewis, acquired from the Steelers in mid-August of 1978 in Knox's second-best trade—Lewis in exchange for the Bills injury prone tight end Paul Seymour, who hated playing in the cold and who was part of the chorus of Bills bitching to be traded. Lewis was brought in by Knox a few days after wide receiver John Holland suffered a season-ending knee injury in an exhibition game against the Browns. The receiving leader in Pittsburgh a few seasons earlier, Lewis would have been a valued starter had the Steelers not possessed two other capable receivers by the names of Lynn Swann and John Stallworth. Lewis became Butler's mentor, teaching him little tricks like how widening his stance and using double moves at the line could help him get up the field in tight coverage. Butler and Lewis gave the Bills their best aerial threat since Ahmad Rashad was traded in 1976.

Knox still had a long way to go in 1979. As has been pointed out, no defense had ever done as feeble a job of stopping the run as the 1978 Bills unit, an ill-equipped 4–3 scheme Knox and Tom Catlin brought over from L.A. The Bills allowed an average of 201.8 rushing yards per game. No team has had as high an average since. In one game against the Browns, the Bills surrendered 309 yards on the ground, including a combined 260 gained by the unrelated Pruitts, Greg and Mike. One significant chink in the Bills frontal armor was Phil Dokes, the disappointing No. 1 pick in 1977 out of Oklahoma State who struggled in 10 games at right defense end in 1978 before dislocating his shoulder.

Determined to plug the middle of the defense, Knox switched to a 3–4 in 1979 to better suit his personnel. By the end of the 1980s, some 25 of 28 NFL teams would use the 3–4 as a base defense.

Knox's second campaign with the Bills was speckled with more positive signs. The team's record improved to 7–9. Rookie Jerry Butler had a career day in Week 4 against the Jets when he caught four touchdowns in the first half. Lean, not afraid to go up for the ball and in possession of prototypical soft hands, Butler set a record for receiving yards (255) that September afternoon while Ferguson threw for 367 yards in a throttling of the Jets, 46–31.

By Week 6 of 1979 the Bills were 3–3 and a game out of first place behind the Dolphins and Patriots, who were tied with 4–2 records. Heading into the third-to-last game, the Bills were still technically in playoff contention at 7–6. They'd just come off a nail-biting 16–13 win over the Patriots at Schaefer Stadium, the first overtime victory in Bills history (OT being implemented in 1974). Fergy had tied it with 11 seconds left with an 11-yard touchdown pass to scrappy third-string receiver Lou Piccone. But in an equally tight contest against the Broncos at Rich Stadium the next week, the Bills lost 19–16 on the last play of the game, a 32-yard Jim Turner field goal which eliminated the Bills from playoff contention.

Flirting with the post-season seemed absurd in Buffalo anyway, but Bills fans were realizing that for the first time in a long while the Bills had a defense. Credit Knox. His decision to switch to the 3–4 paid off. While the Bills may have lacked size up front, they were sitting on an abundance of gifted linebackers, quick, ferocious hitters, like Lucius Sanford, who'd recorded more than 100 tackles in each of his first two seasons, Shane Nelson, who led the team in tackles, and veteran Isiah Robertson, exiled from the Rams that summer. But the rising star linebacker in 1979 was Jim Haslett.

The 6'3", 232-pound Haslett, playing the left inside linebacker slot Knox had envisioned for Cousineau, came up with 13 solo tackles in his first NFL game against the Dolphins. In that thriller against the Patriots that kept the Bills in contention later that season, it was Haslett who intercepted two Steve Grogan passes, including one in overtime that set up the winning drive. Haslett was a renegade, a hell-raiser who, like Knox, had been belched out of the Steel Valley. Haslett grew up in Avalon, Pa. (population 5,250) just outside of Pittsburgh. In college, at Indiana University of Pennsylvania, Haslett was known to beat up rich kids and uproot street signs for fun. On the football field, Haslett's team, the IUP Big Indians, competing in the Pennsylvania Conference, endured three straight losing years playing teams from Slippery Rock and Lock Haven. Of course, Haslett led his team in tackles, while also handling punting duties, once booting a 73-yarder in a game against Lock Haven his senior year.

During his first year in the NFL, Haslett got into dozens of fights. He got into a fight on each of his first two days of practice with the Bills. At night, whether in Buffalo or on the road, Haslett couldn't avoid trouble. Built like an Adonis and afraid of no one, Haslett's cocky, "who dare fuck with me" attitude never sat well with rough and rowdy South Buffalo boys who in the wee hours would venture lit from the legendary Ounce and a Half tavern on Abbott Road and over to the Pierce Arrow in West Seneca, where all the Bills players used to hang out. When there were no South Buffalo guys around to fight, Haslett fought Smerlas.

On the last day of the 1979 season, the Bills traveled to Three Rivers Stadium to face the Pittsburgh Steelers, in

the midst of their Steel Curtain dynasty. Terry Bradshaw, Franco Harris and Mean Joe Greene dominated
the league. The Steelers, peaking and on the verge of
their fourth Super Bowl win in six years, were scarily
proficient, moving up and down the field unencumbered en route to a 28–0 victory, scoring one touchdown
in every frame. In the second quarter, with the Bills trailing 14–0, Steelers quarterback Terry Bradshaw, whom
Haslett had admired while growing up, scrambled out
of bounds and crashed so hard his helmet popped off.
Bringing up the rear on the play was Haslett, who
looked down and saw Bradshaw's head, sans toupee,
poised like a golf ball on a tee. So Haslett intentionally
extended his right foot out a step further than what
would have come naturally and clipped Bradshaw's
forehead with half a cleat, grazing his scalp, and leaving
him with a brush burn and a little trickle of blood. The
ref was right there and pointed at him immediately,
yelling, "You're out!" Haslett was ejected from the game
for unsportsmanlike conduct. At once all of Three
Rivers wanted to kill Jim Haslett and took out their hos-
tilities by picking fights with anyone in the stands un-
lucky enough to be wearing Bills paraphernalia. To the
Steelers fans, Haslett's slip of the cleat was outright des-
ecration. To Bills fans watching on TV it was a promising young player fired up in a meaningless game.

The truth was the Bills didn't belong on the same field
with the Steelers. Afterwards, the Pittsburgh team, having won their division, walked off in a businesslike
manner, the class of the league. The Bills players just
watched, surprised the Steelers were so nonchalant at
having won their division.

Despite the Bills newly potent passing attack, Knox

remained passionate about running the football, early and often. The Bills starting running back, Terry Miller, despite flashes of greatness, had a mediocre 1979 season, notching just 484 yards on 139 carries, and one touchdown. Finishing the season with only 1,621 total team rushing yards, fewest in the entire league, the Bills ground game had hit a post-O.J. funk. Nevertheless, on Draft Day, April 29, 1980, the Bills were not in the market for a running back, instead using their first-round pick to grab Jim Ritcher, a 6'3", 245-pound center from North Carolina State and winner of the Outland Trophy for the nation's most outstanding lineman.

But in the second round, Knox and his scouting director Norm Pollom were miffed to see that Joe Cribbs, a compact, stocky-legged halfback from Auburn whom they had viewed as the second best running back in the draft behind Billy Simms, was still available. They grabbed him, 29th overall, using up the last remaining pick of the five picks obtained from the 49ers in the Simpson trade. Questions surrounding Cribbs' size (5'11", 190) and hence durability, may have contributed to his inconspicuousness on draft day. The fact that Auburn was on NCAA probation and had been barred from Bowl games and television appearances also likely lowered his profile. Knox wasn't worried about his size, joking to Cribbs in their first meeting that "a football doesn't weigh that much."

Cribbs was used to people underestimating him. Born and raised in rural Sulligent, Alabama, a town of less than 3,000 people located about two hours west of Birmingham, Cribbs was always the smallest kid in school, but he was a natural running back. Cribbs started on his high school varsity team as a freshman. He idolized Johnny

Rogers, the 1972 Heisman-winning wingback from Nebraska. Cribbs once scored six touchdowns in one game and had a seventh called back for a penalty. He rarely fumbled. In high school, he went 600 straight carries without a fumble. In college, playing out of the wishbone, Cribbs coughed it up only five times. Though go figure as a rookie with the Bills he would break the franchise record for most fumbles in a season (16).

During the 1980 off-season, the Bills traded receiver Bobby Chandler, best known for his ridiculous circus catches, like the tippy-toe tightrope one he made in the back of the end zone against Tampa Bay. With movie star looks, Chandler had played with O.J. at USC, and wanted to return to the West Coast, maybe even get his feet wet in television broadcasting. As kids we loved to pretend we were Chandler, tossing footballs to ourselves and leaning out over an imaginary sideline. But the truth was Chandler was constantly moaning about the cold weather in Buffalo. He went to the Raiders. For Chandler we got Phil Villapiano, aging, a few steps slower, but an inspirational veteran leader and blue-collar, beer-drinking kind of guy who brought with him a brand of heart and emotion the Bills fans had never seen. We'd traded a "Hollywood" type for more of a true Buffalonian.

Villapiano was a native of Bruce Springsteen's hometown of Asbury Park, New Jersey, and there was little question he was born to stop the run. Though he played standout defensive end at Bowling Green, NFL scouts ignored Villapiano, viewed him as undersized (6'1", 222). So in the 1971 Senior Bowl Villapiano switched to linebacker. His aggressive style in that game impressed Raiders owner Al Davis enough to draft him in the second round.

He would start his rookie season, and would appear in four Pro Bowls (1973–76). In 1977, Villapiano was a key part of the Raiders team that beat the Minnesota Vikings in the Super Bowl, even forcing a goal line fumble.

Not long after the 1977 Super Bowl win, Al Davis announced that he was moving the Raiders to Los Angeles at the end of the 1980 season. Villapiano was quoted in an Oakland paper saying that he wouldn't go. Davis never forgot this. He called Villapiano at his home one Sunday morning in early April of 1980 and asked him what he knew about Bills receiver Bobby Chandler. Villapiano had played with Chandler on some Pro Bowl teams and vouched for him. "Good guy, great player Al. So who do the Bills want for him?"

"You," Davis said, and with that fulfilled Villapiano's prophecy.

In that same off-season Knox claimed beefy Colts fullback Roosevelt Leaks off waivers for blocking and short yardage situations, and to provide a solid backup to Curtis Brown, a decent fullback entering his fourth year with the team.

When the Bills entered camp just 15 players remained from the 1977 squad that Knox inherited, including Ben Williams, who worked as a loan officer at a Jackson, Mississippi bank during the off-season, and safety Charles Romes, a 12th-round pick in 1977 who played only one year of college ball at North Carolina Central. Young talent was abundant. While all three of Knox's number-one draft picks in 1978, 1979 and 1980 would be non-factors in the 1980 campaign (Terry Miller would lose his starting job to Cribbs, Cousineau had split for the CFL and Ritcher sat the bench playing behind Will

Grant), a total of 18 players from those drafts remained on the roster, nine of them starters.

Entering camp, the last major links to the O.J. Simpson era remaining on the Bills were McKenzie and Ferguson, as well as tight end Reuben Gant, free safeties Tony Greene and Steve Freeman, defensive tackle Mike Kadish and five-time All-Pro guard Joe DeLamielleure.

DeLamielleure had demanded to be traded that spring. A familiar story Buffalonians had heard before: a star Bills player feeling disrespected, frustrated with losing, tired of Buffalo, insisting on a trade. De-Lamielleure was a tough player, a perfect fit with working-class Buffalo and a guy who should have gotten along just fine with Chuck Knox. A native of Detroit, DeLamielleure was ninth out of 10 kids. His family lived down the street from a Chrysler plant as well as his dad's bar, The Victory Inn. As a result, De-Lamielleure spent much of his teenage years pounding beers and getting in fistfights with autoworkers.

As a rookie in 1973, DeLamielleure was diagnosed by Bills doctors as having a heart condition and was told he might never play football again. "You flunked your physical," a visibly upset Lou Saban told him a few days after the No. 1 pick out of Michigan State arrived in town in late March of '73. Duffy Daugherty, De-Lamielleure's coach at Michigan State, arranged for him to get a second opinion at the Cleveland Clinic in Ohio and within a few minutes of checking his pulse, doctors told him that he'd been misdiagnosed; later on, a heart catharization, at the time a relatively new procedure, showed conclusively there was nothing wrong with him. DeLamielleure was cleared to play by the time camp opened.

That season he would block for O.J. Simpson who blew the nation's mind by cracking the 2,000-yard barrier. DeLamielleure went on to become one of the best offensive linemen in history. The dispute with Knox wasn't about money. Knox wanted DeLamielleure on the team, and certainly his teammates did as well. But De-Lamielleure and Knox had their differences, partly about how offensive line should be played—Knox believed that linemen should square opponents up and lock them in place, and let the running back find the seam, as opposed to DeLamielleure's style of blowing guys off the line of scrimmage. Mostly, though, DeLamielleure didn't like the way Knox placated wild troublemakers like Isiah Robertson, whose hard-partying ways sometimes got out of hand.

Knox refused to trade DeLamielleure. But just to let him know he wasn't frightened of losing him, Knox brought in the notorious Conrad Dobler right before the start of the 1980 training camp, which convened at Niagara University on July 20.

Dobler was a legend of the game, part of the fabled 1975 St. Louis Cardinals offensive line that tied a record for fewest sacks (8) allowed in a season. Dobler, a mustachioed cross between Dick Butkus and Al Capone, endured most of his career maimed by two terribly arthritic knees.

Discarded by the Cards as a busted player at the end of the 1977 season, Dobler next found employment with the New Orleans Saints. In two years on the Saints, Dobler did his part to help the perennial losers start to right their ship. The Saints had never won more than five games in their history, but won 7 games in 1978.

Then the team managed to go 8–8 the following year. That year the Saints allowed the second fewest sack total in the league, just 17.

Not of tremendous build (6'3", 255) Dobler could barely walk from his knee injuries and surgical repairs that spanned back to his high school days. A native of Twentynine Palms, California, near Palm Springs, Dobler grew up the fourth of seven children born to a milk distributor serving tiny towns in the Mojave Desert. Dobler, a star halfback in high school, was recruited to the University of Wyoming as a tight end and eventually transformed into an offensive tackle. A fifth-round pick in the 1972 draft, Dobler was released by the Cardinals before the start of what would have been his first season. But when a first-stringer went down with a pre-season injury, the 22-year-old was brought back. He vowed privately to make the most of the reprieve.

During his six years in St. Louis, Dobler forged a reputation for viciousness to rival Ivan the Terrible's. Dobler was once summoned to Pete Rozelle's office on Park Avenue in New York for an official "shape up or ship out" sitdown at which time the former NFL Commissioner played a highlight reel of Dobler throwing elbows to the throat, kicking guys, kneeing them and of course, employing his patented leg whip. "We just can't have this kind of thing in the NFL," Rozelle told him.

Dobler wore extra shin pads taped to his calves. When a defensive lineman tried to throw Dobler aside, he tapped into the centrifugal forces being used against him and with a violent, tripping motion, his leg came whirling back around like a numchuck.

Dobler was nasty. His entire modus operandi involved getting inside an opponent's head, making them so angry at him that they'd often blow assignments, lose focus. When a defensive lineman jumped up to bat down a pass, Dobler would often come with a signature double-fisted uppercut to the solar plexus. Somehow deflecting passes didn't carry the same importance after that. He sometimes gouged throats. Dobler once made a grown NFL lineman break down and cry during a game.

"One of these days someone is going to break Dobler's neck, and I'm not going to send any flowers," said Merlin Olsen, the Rams star lineman who loathed Dobler's tactics. An interesting choice of words, considering that in addition to "Father Murphy" he would later go on to star in a slew of FTD commercials. As Father Murphy, Olsen once had a tombstone created as a prop for a cemetery scene that read "Here Lies Conrad Dobler, Gone but Not Forgiven."

Dobler became infamous for biting, though he always swore his teeth marks were only embedded into the flesh of a single player, Doug Sutherland, of the Minnesota Vikings, who made the mistake of sticking his fingers through Dobler's facemask. It was a *Monday Night Football* game in 1974 and afterwards, a straight-faced Sutherland told a reporter that he had to request a rabies shot because he'd been bitten by Conrad Dobler.

Some of his reputation as the dirtiest player in football was manufactured by opponents and stoked by the media, but a lesser known quality was Dobler's ability to motivate. He was inspiration in cleats; by his sheer obliviousness to pain and adversity, Dobler, perpetually battling, leaving everything on the field, could show players with two good legs how anything was possible. He expected a lot from people and took it upon himself to ride his fellow lineman, fining them $5 for each sack, and calling them out on even the least bit of ass dragging.

Not afraid to speak his mind, Dobler took Ferguson aside early in camp after watching some films. It was clear that oftentimes Fergy held the ball too long. He had been sacked 43 times in 1979.

"When you get sacked, the linemen, they think it's their fault and now they start playing scared all day," Dobler explained one early July evening as he and Fergy sat in the AV department at Dunleavy Hall, the only building at Niagara with air conditioning. "Just get rid of it."

That summer Dobler and Villapiano roomed together at camp. They had become the ringleaders when it came to extracurricular activities, ranging from harmless after-lunch water gun attacks on rookie players as they napped in the O'Shea dorms to all-night beer blasts at The Old San Juan, a dive bar in one of the more seedy parts of Niagara Falls not far from the Love Canal section, a ten-block ghost town from which hundreds of families had been frantically forced to evacuate two summers earlier because of toxic waste.

In the summer of 1980, a New York State Assembly Task Force was hearing testimony from former residents and Hooker Chemical executives to try to get to the bottom of why chemical waste had been dumped in the Love Canal area in the 1940s. It turned out Hooker was working for Uncle Sam during World War II, and ultimately the federal government would take responsibility for the mess.

My older sister Patsy attended Niagara. That summer she was between her sophomore and junior years, taking chemistry courses and working part-time on campus. Patsy got to know some of the Bills. The rumor in my neighborhood a summer earlier was that she was dating one of the Bills linemen, the sultan of holding-penalties, Ken Jones. Jones got flagged so much that Knox had his number changed from 73 to 72 (which belonged to tackle Jon Borchardt) midway through the 1978 season in an attempt to lower his profile with the referees. But if it worked, it had more to do with Jones being mortified than with Knox's chicanery. Also, just to set the record straight, he never did date my sister.

One carefree summer day Patsy took me to see the Bills at training camp. It was a hot day—that whole summer had been hotter than usual—and about all I can remember was trying to get running back Curtis Brown's autograph. Brown, who tooled around Niagara that summer in a gold Corvette, was one of the last of the Bills to hang around and oblige autograph seekers after practice. I waited and waited but I never did get his signature. I also vaguely remember someone with curly black hair (which was probably Villapiano) being jovial on the sidelines in a red perforated half-jersey.

By the end of the first few weeks of camp, Knox was showing he was determined to prune away old links to losing times. Phil Dokes, who had missed the entire 1979 season, walked out of camp July 30th, telling his Tulsa-based agent Wes Ellsworth that he wanted to be traded. Knox didn't care what Dokes did—as far as he was concerned his career was over. Veteran free safety Tony Greene, just three interceptions away from becoming the Bills all-time leader, was waived. So was Willie Parker, three-year starter at center.

Bent on purging the Bills of players overly conditioned to losing, Knox was cleaning house, loading up on new blood. Twelve rookies would make the 1980 squad.

The season was drawing closer. For diehard baseball fans, there's the annual ritual of counting down the days until pitchers and catchers report to training camp. For diehard Bills fans, there's the Cleveland scrimmage.

The Bills brought 69 players to the scrimmage against the Browns held Sunday, August 3, in a drizzle at Kent State University. Ferguson was excited to test out the new shotgun formation, but it was the Bills rushing attack that had Knox smiling at the end of the game. Even though the Bills lost 6–0, their eight running backs gained 225 yards on 43 attempts, or around five yards a crack. Cribbs had seven carries for 37 yards. A year earlier, no Bill had rushed for more than 100 yards in a game; the Bills as a team barely rushed for a 100 yards a game, ranking dead last in the AFC.

When the scrimmage was over Knox stood on the sidelines, puffing a cigar and gulping a cold beer. "I liked what I saw today," he told Dobler, who'd done a stellar job paving lanes on the right side of the field. "That Cribbs is going to be a great one."

The following Saturday, the eyes of the nation, emotionally drained by the energy crisis, high inflation and the lingering Iranian hostage situation, were fixed on President Carter bracing for the Democratic National Convention in New York City. As if his plate at the White House wasn't already full enough, Carter had spent the summer fending off allegations that his embarrassing brother was making shady deals with the Libyans, perhaps to sell "Billy" beer. But in the small steel city of Lackawanna, just south of Buffalo, all eyes were on the Bills pre-season opener against the Philadelphia Eagles at nearby Rich Stadium. The 6 P.M. exhibition game had been dubbed "Polish Night with the Polish Rifle" in honor of Lackawanna native Ron Jaworski. After a few seasons playing with Knox on the Rams, Jaworski (a Bills fan growing up in his close-knit Polish neighborhood) had firmly won the starting job for the Eagles. He'd turned in a valiant 1979 campaign in which he started every game, despite a broken finger, severe big toe infections and sprained ligaments in his ankle.

Now in his sixth season, Jaworski was coming back to Buffalo an NFL star and clearly the night belonged to him. The rifleman came out firing and led the Eagles to an early 21–0 lead from which they never looked back. Jaworski went 8 of 11 for 120 yards and one touchdown. It was Knox's ninth straight exhibition game defeat as Bills coach.

In one of the lone bright spots of the game, Fergy tossed a second quarter touchdown pass to rookie tight end Mark Brammer who'd come in to replace Reuben Gant, knocked out of the game with a leg bruise.

But the Bills continued to work hard, enduring two-a-day sessions in the stifling mid-August heat. One day, special teams coach Elijah Pitts asked for volunteers to cover a kickoff toward the end of the day's second session. Tired and miserable, a group of younger players and rookies sat under a tree hoping someone else would accept the role of martyr. When no one got up, Dobler, coming off yet another off-season knee surgery, limped out on the field, and within a minute there was no longer a shortage of volunteers.

At the end of the last practice on the final day of camp

(Friday, August 15th) Knox called the players together and told them he had four kegs of beer on ice for them. "Go on, get hammered. You all earned it," he said over thunderous shouting. That afternoon the players bonded as a team, carrying the party over to the Old San Juan, standing out front, the kings of Western New York, toasting the season ahead. The next evening in Detroit, the Bills lost their 10th straight pre-season game to the Lions 24–17 at the Silverdome.

Ralph Wilson might have been a little agitated to see the Bills commit 14 penalties in front of his hometown, except for the fact that he was still riding the high of a horsebreeding coup staged a couple of weeks earlier. Wilson had sold three of his horses, two fillies and a colt, at the annual Keeneland Yearling Sale in Lexington, Kentucky, for close to a million dollars. Coincidentally, not long after Wilson's windfall, a slew of disgruntled players—such as wide receiver Lou Piccone and defensive end Ben Williams—ended their holdouts and reported for duty.

The Lions, led by rookie rushing sensation Billy Sims, had gained 345 yards, but the Bills defense would redeem itself the following week against the Green Bay Packers visiting Rich Stadium. The Packers, coached by Bart Starr, gained just 130 yards in Knox's first preseason win as Bills coach. But in the final warm-up Earl Campbell and the Houston Oilers pounded the Bills 24–7 on a Thursday night at the Astrodome.

A few days after that game, on Sunday, August 31st one week before the opening game against the Dolphins, the Bills 6'5", 250-pound defensive end Sherman White ended his third holdout in three years. That same day, DeLamielleure announced he was ending his holdout as well, except he never showed up for practice by now being held at Erie Community College South located right across Abbott Road from Rich Stadium. Trade talks were going nowhere. The next day, Monday, Knox called DeLamielleure at 8 A.M. and told him to come into his office for a heart to heart talk. By the end of it they'd each aired their differences. When DeLamielleure asked if a trade could be worked out by the noon deadline, Knox said he didn't think so.

Arriving in the locker room, DeLamielleure saw some handwritten signs players had fashioned welcoming him back. Donning pads, he was about to get on a bus that would take him to the E.C.C.-South practice field, when Norm Pollom told him that Knox wanted to see him once again in his office. The Browns had called just before noon. A deal had been struck, two undisclosed draft picks in exchange for one of the best guards to ever play the position. The Bills only Pro Bowl player was gone.

Predicting the Bills would finish fourth in the AFC East with a 6–10 record, *Sports Illustrated's* Paul Zimmerman (in his second year at the magazine and not yet having earned his "Dr. Z" handle) delivered a scathing scouting report in the "NFL Preview" issue.

"Bad trades helped wreck the once proud Buffalo franchise, and now Chuck Knox is trying to put it back together again," Zimmerman wrote. "Buffalo is patching and groping, picking up older vets like Roosevelt Leaks and Phil Villapiano, hoping to get lucky. Knox suffered a setback when Joe DeLamielleure, the right guard and a five-time Pro Bowl choice, said he'd had it with the Bills . . . so the Bills acquired Conrad Dobler from New Orleans, but Dobler couldn't hack it any longer on his arthritic knees and was cut. And De-Lamielleure was traded to Cleveland."

SI's Zimmerman picked the New England Patriots to win the AFC East at 11–5, followed by the Dolphins and the Jets.

As Knox worked to get down to a 45-man roster by the September 1 deadline, one of his cuts had indeed been Dobler. It was a calculated gamble. Knox quietly placed Dobler on the waiver wire in the hope that no team would take him. If no team claimed Dobler off waivers the Bills could invite him back as a free agent, a move designed to give Knox more flexibility as he whittled down the roster. Dobler, well paid and presumed to be shot, went unclaimed. Knox quickly re-signed him.

The next day, 230-pound fullback Dennis Johnson, in his third season with the Bills out of Mississippi State, was released. His job backing up starting fullback Curtis Brown went to the ex-Colt, "older vet" Rosie Leaks. Ex-Seahawk receiver Duke Fergerson, who'd been waived two days earlier, was brought back as the Bills fifth receiver behind Lewis, Butler, Ram import Ron Jessie and Piccone. Odd man out was receiver Danny "Steam Machine" Fulton, who'd only caught two passes for 34 yards in two seasons with the Bills. A few days before the roster was finalized, Fulton was sent packing to his hometown Omaha, Nebraska where he took up selling vacuum cleaners, only to resurface for a couple of seasons with the Browns.

Rookie quarterback prospect Gene Bradley, who'd been drafted by Knox in the second round out of Arkansas State as a possible heir apparent to Ferguson, was also released. Backing up Ferguson would be Dan Manucci in just his second year with the team out of

Kansas State, while 28-year-old David Humm would be the third-string QB.

Rookie punter Greg Cater, a 10th round pick out of Tennessee-Chattanooga, was among the last to be signed, bringing the roster to 45 men.

Dobler and Villapiano, who drove to and from practice together every day in Villapiano's truck, were chatting on the way home that Friday before the Miami game.

"It's just like when I was on the Saints," Dobler said. "They got so used to losing no one knew what it was like to win. If we can just teach these younger guys how to be winners, I'm telling you this could be one hell of a year."

"I think you're right," said Villapiano, speeding along Big Tree Road in Orchard Park. "I think we got something going here."

CHAPTER THREE

5–0

The stories of the Rich Stadium goal posts being torn down after the historic opening game against the Dolphins spread around town in paths almost as circuitous as the ones taken by the two sets of uprights themselves. In three-dollar backyard parking lots and dimly lit taverns up and down Abbott Road, gloriously drunk fans recounted tales of rushing the field, all of them boasting to have been "right there." Like an army of ants on an accidentally discarded ice cream bar, the rowdy Bills end zone rapidly filled in at the base of the stanchion, while a few fans climbed on to the crossbar. One guy managed to shimmy all the way up to the top of one of the posts, and for perhaps 20 seconds or so he hung on triumphantly, his sun visor sliding down over his face like a surgical mask. Not long after his fleeting, victorious moment in time, the posts buckled over and he was swallowed up by the throng.

The frenetic mob stormed down the length of the field carrying one set of posts as if they were a battering ram, eventually charging back up into the stands, to the highest row of seats in the nosebleed section, and then tossed the posts over the side down to a crowd of fans below. Across the stadium, a second cadre of overzealous fans tried to present the other set of goal posts to

Bills owner Ralph Wilson, only they couldn't possibly fit the monster yellow tines into his luxury box, a logistical snag which should have seemed obvious to someone at the time.

Wilson had been branded by most Buffalonians as too tight with the purse strings, but after the Miami game, he was more than happy to pay for a new set of posts, which at the time cost around $3,000 each.

That next Monday morning, as I seem to recall it, a local disc jockey was describing the mad scene at the game when some still exhilarated fans called in to say they had wound up with one of the goal posts. The deejay convinced them to come to the station and later a sizeable chunk was shaved into souvenir rings to raise money for charity.

The win over the Dolphins had captured the city's attention, even if the rest of the country was pretty much oblivious. On *Monday Night Football* half time highlights, Howard Cosell didn't even mention the game or show any footage. No matter. Just as the rare but appreciated Indian summer weather seemed to linger in Western New York that September, Bills euphoria did too—because something totally unexpected happened.

The Bills kept winning.

In Week 2, Rich Stadium played host to the re-emerging New York Jets, viewed by many around the league as being on the cusp of a breakout year. The Jets had finished 8–8 the prior season, but led the NFL in rushing yards. Not one of their running backs cracked 1,000 yards in 1979, but the quartet of Clark Gaines, Scott Dierking, Kevin Long and Bruce Harper had combined for nearly 2,400 on the back of outstanding offensive tackle Marvin Powell. Quarterback Richard Todd was considered a rising star in the league, as was his primary receiver Wesley Walker.

A special half time ceremony had been planned to induct O.J. Simpson as the first member of the newly created Bills Wall of Fame. Earlier that week, down at City Hall, Mayor Jimmy Griffin had officially designated it "O.J. Week" in Buffalo. During a staged photo op, Reggie McKenzie hoisted the fiery, diminutive mayor into his arms like he was a crayon, while a beaming Griffin signed into effect a declaration of O.J. Simpson. Erie County Executive Ed Rutkowski, a former Bill, as well as team marketing chief Pat McGroder, were also on hand.

On the Friday afternoon before the Jets game, the Bills gathered for a players-only powwow held in the general meeting room back behind the trainer's area in the bowels of the stadium. A de facto veteran leadership council of Ferguson, McKenzie, Shane Nelson, as well as new vets Dobler and Villapiano, had sprung up, and the younger guys, rookies, rejects, second- and third-year players just trying to survive in the NFL, were more than inclined to listen to them. It had been McKenzie's initiative to start holding these meetings, although Knox, seeing the camaraderie that was developing, arranged for a raft of pizzas to be delivered.

"There hasn't been any pride up here in Buffalo for a while," Dobler told his teammates when given a turn to speak. "We have to change that."

These weren't empty platitudes meant to supply theatrics for some NFL Films segment. Dobler knew how to motivate, having been part of respected Cardinals teams that topped the NFC East in the early 1970s. Dobler had really lit a fire under the Bills offensive line, which against the Dolphins did not allow a single sack or commit a single penalty.

"Let's just keep winning," Villapiano chimed in. "The only way you get that pride is by winning."

The morning of the game, September 14, 1980, after finishing my *Courier-Express* paper route, I thumbed out to the stadium along with two of my best friends, Pat Keane and John Fischer. Rich Stadium was five miles away, a straight shot down Abbott Road, and rides were generally easy to come by, as someone from the neighborhood who either knew us, our dads, or one of our brothers, usually obliged. That day we snuck into the stadium compliments of my neighbor, Mr. Greene, a Bethlehem Steel worker who'd just recently been laid off, and was taking tickets. While it was hard to see him through the crowd, once I sheepishly made eye contact with him his friendly glance eased us through the turnstile. The excitement of our entry into the Rich Stadium maelstrom gave way to anticipation as we joined in the raucous march of the Buffalo faithful.

I suppose it would be unheard of today for a bunch of 12-year-old kids to sneak unchaperoned into a major sporting event, let alone hitchhike there, but back then it was no big deal, at least it didn't seem that way to me, although Pat and Fish likely did not tell their moms what we were up to. I wouldn't have needed anyone's permission.

For a seventh-grader I was enjoying exceedingly rare freedom. At the time, my mother was in Mercy Hospital suffering from complications after a wicked gall bladder surgery, while my dad had just been ejected from the house, flagged by mom for excessive carousal. With my older sister Patsy away at Niagara University and my older brother Tommy battling the hardships of cerebral palsy, that left only one babysitter for me and my brother Shawn (eleven months younger), and that was our oldest brother Danny, who'd just graduated from Canisius College. Danny had crashed two cars that summer, including mom's, and lived at home as he struggled to find a job in the recession. He worked the Jets game that day as an usher.

It rained on and off all day but it was warm out. My buddies and I shuffled around the stadium looking for seats, eventually opting to kneel along the stairwell in an area just diagonal to the end zones, which we would later come to call "Old Faithful." Whenever we couldn't find seats for ourselves, these long, wide concrete ramparts afforded us an unencumbered view of the field. Old Faithful had no ushers, and plenty of room for people to step around us, so no one ever complained. It was almost like our own private box.

My brother worked in the section right under Ralph Wilson's luxury suite. This section was almost all season ticket holders who knew exactly how to get to their seats, so Danny never really had to do much.

Just before the end of the first half, Ferguson led an aggressive hurryup drive out of the shotgun in a game the Bills were winning 7–3, their lone score coming on a one-yard Joe Cribbs dive over the top. The Cribbs touchdown had been set up by a 48-yard screen pass to Reuben Gant in one of the biggest gains of his career. Ferguson had dropped back, deeper than usual, rolling toward the far right, but then he turned and fired a rocket across the width of the field to Gant who followed Ken Jones down the left sideline, cut back into the middle of the field before being dragged down by Jets defensive back Darrol Ray at the 2.

As the first half wound down, Ferguson hit on consecutive pass completions, allowing kicker Nick Mike-Mayer to boot a 47-yarder. The crowd was delighted, but it wasn't so much the three points as it was a collective acknowledgment that times were changing for the better. The old Bills would have just knelt with 40 seconds to play in the half, wholly content to head into the locker room with a secure lead. These were the new Bills, using their new shotgun.

During half time the fans celebrated the Bills of old with a hearty tribute to Simpson, the first name enshrined on the Wall of Fame. The Juice was rolled out to midfield in a golf cart, and to this day I can still see him, wearing a red blazer, smiling, waving to the adoring fans.

It was a bittersweet moment for everyone. O.J. had played for nine mostly remarkable seasons in Buffalo during the 1970s. Simpson's first game with the Bills was in 1969 on this same date, September 14, against this same team, the New York Jets. Before the game Joe Namath wished the young Heisman winner good luck. The Bills, quarterbacked by James Harris, lost, 33–19. My father, an usher that day at sold-out War Memorial Stadium, shot cherished 8-mm home movies of O.J. warming up before kickoff.

Simpson's last game was October 30, 1977, a 4 P.M. televised road game against the Seattle Seahawks, the pathetic expansion team which was added to the league along with the equally lame Tampa Bay Buccaneers in 1976. This loss to the Seahawks is quite possibly the most humiliating defeat in Bills history, a 56–17 drubbing to a team that didn't even exist a year-and-a-half earlier. Statistically, it proved to be the worst defensive performance the Bills ever produced, as the Seahawks amassed 559 total yards.

I followed the travesty whilst trick-or-treating in my little Covington Gardens neighborhood in West Seneca. Part of St. Martin's Parish, Covington Gardens—just five streets, Covington, Tudor, Tampa, Woodcrest, Brookside—was among the first subdivisions built just south of Buffalo in the late 1950s, a fairly basic enclave of tree-lined streets jammed with brightly colored two-story wooden houses. For some reason never thoroughly explained to me, the night before Halloween (known as Beggar's Night) was deemed by the Town of West Seneca as the official night for candy solicitation. Just a few streets away in South Buffalo, trick-or-treating took place on the night of Halloween itself, so growing up we could fill our pillowcases with candy on back-to-back nights. On Beggar's Night 1977, I was dressed up as the hunchback of Notre Dame, the Robertsons and Gallivans, bums. We trotted along together from house to house, up Tudor toward Potter Road, as the state of the Bills-Seahawks game kept getting worse. As we collected our candy at the front doors of homes with the lights on (we never "tricked" the darkened homes, which is not to say my friends and I weren't capable of despicable acts of vandalism on occasion), we could see the people watching on TV inside continue to grow angrier and more disgusted, until finally in one living room on the far end of Tudor, I could see O.J. being helped off the field. "Lost for the season," the adults were saying, as they bestowed us with Mallow Cups and mini-Baby Ruths. While we didn't know it at the time, he would never suit up in a Bills uniform again.

Now Simpson was officially retired at age 33. He'd

just started his own film production company, Orenthal
Productions, inking a deal with NBC to do a slew of
made-for-TV movies.

Simpson gave a short speech to a hushed Rich Stadium crowd. He insisted that even though his career
wrapped up in San Francisco, he'd left his heart in Buffalo. "I take pride in knowing that I have the acceptance
and respect of the people in Buffalo," he told the appre-
ciative fans. Right at that moment, as he wiped a tear
from his eye, blinking out at the sea of spectators in red,
white and blue, Simpson couldn't have foreseen what
lay head of him: a sequel to "Goldie and the Boxer;" his
hilarious part as Norberg in the "Naked Gun" films; a
prime gig with NBC Sports as a sideline reporter cover-
ing the AFC; infamy.

By the start of the second half my buddies and I found
better seats down in the lower rows of the Jets end zone
section, so we had a great view of safety Jeff Nixon returning an interception 50 yards for a touchdown with a
minute left in the third quarter. The Bills ended up winning 20–10, the Jets lone touchdown coming on a meaningless 11-yard Todd pass to Clark Gaines with three
seconds to play. For the second week in a row, the defense held their opponent to just one touchdown. For
only the second time in 15 years, the Bills started off a
season with two wins.

"Proud Bills Throttle Jets" was the headline in the
sports page of the *Courier-Express* the next day, with the
lead story quoting Joe Ferguson on the importance of
Dobler and Villapiano's pep talk a few days earlier.
"They've been with winners before," Fergy said. "Now
we are developing pride here."

Once again, Ferguson had not been sacked. He spent

the day grinding out first downs via screen passes and short tosses over the middle. Cribbs and Leaks combined for 100 yards on the ground.

Because I was a *Courier-Express* paperboy, I somehow felt privileged that I was the first one to glimpse the treasure that was the Monday morning sports page after a win. It would be just after 6:00 A.M., dark and brisk, and from the storm door where I waited, I could hear the noisy *Courier* truck rumble down Tudor Boulevard. I'd watch it lurch to a halt in front of my house. Three big bundles of newspapers would be slung into the pine green wooden chest at the end of the driveway, and then the truck would zip over to the Gallivan driveway to make a drop in their paperbox. I'd clip open the taut yellow plastic strips that held the issues in bundles, and then tear apart the first shredded newspaper on top to get the second one below's sports page, and there it would be, the banner headline proclaiming victory and the final score.

As the Bills winning streak continued, those scores got more impressive.

In Week 3, the Bills beat Archie Manning and the New Orleans Saints, 35–26, in the Superdome, site of the next Super Bowl. The 0–2 Saints, among the worst teams in NFL history (they would win one game in 1980) were *favored* to beat the Bills by two points. True, the Saints were coming off an 8–8 season in 1979, but during the 1970s, pitiful play in The Big Easy drove fans to wearing paper bags on their heads, possibly providing the inspiration for The Unknown Comic on "The Gong Show."

I watched the Saints game on the color TV in my basement along with Timmy Gallivan from across the street. It was a rare achievement for the Bills to put up five touchdowns. Ferguson had tried a long bomb on the very first play of the game, and although he failed to connect, symbolically it spoke volumes and got us fired up. Eventually, Frank Lewis hauled in a pair of touchdown grabs with his big long fingers. That day, Lewis collected six catches for 82 yards. Ferguson finally did connect on a big pass to Butler, a 69-yarder, to this day the fourth longest, non-scoring reception in Bills history. Butler snagged five passes for 133 yards. Cribbs ran for 90 yards, caught 3 balls for 36 yards, and scored two touchdowns.

The Saints actually led at the half, 19–14, with 10 of their points coming off two Ferguson interceptions. To watch the Bills come out in the second half, shrug off adversity, take the lead, pull away strong—it was all way too unrealistic, but there it was, happening, on my basement TV screen. The Bills sealed that win against the Saints with a 92-yard touchdown drive that chewed up most of the fourth quarter. The defense had held the Saints to just 38 yards rushing that day. After the game, it was unmistakable—the Bills were for real.

As a kid, watching the Bills play on television was as good as going to the game, perhaps even better, mainly because as much as I loved going to the games, I also truly loved watching TV. And nothing, not "SWAT," nor "Happy Days," nor an R-rated Home Box Office flick, not even a stolen Friday night "Monty Python" on PBS could even remotely compare to the bliss that I experienced when watching the Bills play on the tube. Since games never sold out in time to lift the local television blackout, it was only during those eight away-game Sundays that me and my friends could watch the Bills from the familiar confines of my basement or the Gallivan family room. We watched a lot of football growing up, but we played a lot too. "Bills Fever" electrified the Tudor Football League.

Unlike the Bills, the TFL flourished during the 1970s. But in 1980 it too was entering a new phase. The league's beginnings can be traced back to the early 1970s, when the oldest kids on Tudor—my brother Danny, Ronnie Boss, the Kennedy brothers, Billy, Tommy and Boogsie—used house paint to mark the lines and hash marks of an entire 100-yard football field on the blacktop of our street, all of it painstakingly tape-measured. The next generation of kids—Mike Greene, Mike Gallivan, Mike Holdren, Pat Murtha, John Boss—re-did the field sometime around 1975, painting an authentic Buffalo Bills helmet midfield. It was white, with a navy blue, red-striped charging Buffalo, done to match the new Bills emblem instituted in 1974 which replaced the old, simple, bright red, stripeless Buffalo. Billy Kennedy, by this time long retired from TFL, took the time to hand paint that Bills helmet, right in front of the Greene's house. Not long after that Billy would be paralyzed in an automobile accident. His craftsmanship was top-notch, but fell victim to sabotage before the paint even dried when my nervy brother Shawn purposely skidded on his banana-seat bike across the freshly adorned concrete, immediately becoming a fugitive in the neighborhood. An angry posse spearheaded by Mike Greene was organized, as Shawn fled on two paint-smudged wheels, a faint trail of red, white and blue in his wake. Shawn's rebellious smudge across the painted helmet was only partially reparable, and the entire incident earned him a lifetime TFL suspension, later overturned.

Shawnie would continue to rock the boat, capriciously flaunting TFL's no-punting conventions put in place for ball security during road games, meaning those games played at Potter Road Elementary School (the roof of which is probably still littered with footballs booted from Shawn's toe despite our repeated warnings).

We took our game to Potter whenever we felt the urge for tackle football, or had too many players for a street game, or when our neighbor, Mr. Paradowski, angrily chased us off Tudor, usually after an errant throw thudded off the roof of his car. The grumpy, pipe-smoking Polishman would chastise us regularly for playing in the street when nearby there was the gigantic Potter Road field. As noted, Potter was good for a big tackle game, but for four on four, nothing beat Tudor.

The big-time, two-hand touch street games played on Tudor were real happenings, as kids from South Buffalo, like the Turner and Carlyle crews, came to play our team, the "Tudor Trojans." My younger gang, consisting of myself, my brother Shawn, Matty Greene, Mikey Robertson and Timmy Gallivan, could only play on the official field when the older kids weren't using it.

The first of us younger guys welcomed into the big show was Matty Greene, who happened to be the smallest kid on the block, but a natural athlete. A story had gone around Tudor that before a Bills game Mr. Greene had arranged for Matty to meet O.J. in the tunnel, and I can still remember being floored by the tale. Mikey Robertson was next to join his older brothers, Timmy and Larry, in the big time games.

The single most talented TFL touch football player of the golden era was John Boss, a.k.a "Bossy." Never before or since have I seen someone bend, contort, twist and scamper out of the way of human hands that needed merely touch him to stop his progress, the way Bossy did. Bossy could break away at will, at any time, especially on kickoffs, and when he finally was stopped it involved an endless series of spine-flailing, neck-bending maneuvers. Bossy, who would go on to be a star golfer at Bishop Timon High School, solidified his reputation as neighborhood God when in 1978 he famously got kicked out of St. Martin's School after hurling a pile of textbooks (along with a few choice words) at our intimidating principal, Sister Mary Eyemard.

By 1980 the town of West Seneca had paved over the once epic Tudor field, faded and illegible from years of winter erosion. Homeowners were put on notice by the Town of West Seneca Public Works Department that a repeat rendition was unwelcome. The TFL game changed dramatically, moving down Tudor, closer to my house at the corner of Maryon. We shifted to a telephone pole to telephone pole setup, a much shorter field lengthwise, except now it was wider, on account of all the ditches on Tudor having been removed and smoothed over with grass. Games normally involved a cast of eight regular players: myself, my brother Shawn, the three Robertson brothers, Timmy, Larry and Mikey, and the three Gallivan brothers, Timmy, John and Mike. Mike Gallivan, an elder during the heyday, was among the last links to the golden era. Bossy, by this time preoccupied with golf or more grown up adventures, would make only the rarest appearances. Matty Greene, likewise, was also busy with "real" sports, becoming an accomplished hockey player for the best area travel teams.

The Downey brothers, Bobby and Jimmy, and the Barretts, Mike and Matt, were semi-regulars. There was

also the occasional presence of John "Skitch" Hender-
son, a lanky, brillo-haired neighborhood punk who
went to the public West Seneca West High School, as opposed to private Catholic Timon. Skitch smoked ciga-
rettes, shoplifted, knew where to get fireworks, showed
us porno magazines—it was Skitch who told me there
was no Santa Claus. Skitch and I once fought on his
garage roof on a hot summer afternoon as practically
the entire neighborhood watched from below. The
crowd cried for mercy when he delivered a crushing,
military-style death blow to my throat as I lay sprawled
on my back under a blazing sun.

In 1980, TFL was ruled by the Robertson brothers.
They were all good players. Mikey, in fact, would go on
to play quarterback at Timon, and for Canisius College.
The Robertsons were always last to arrive for games
held after supper on school nights, around 5:45 P.M., but
when they did show they brought the necessary enthu-
siasm for a competitive, enjoyable affair, obtainable at
least two-thirds of the time. But the slightest thing—an
odd number of players, or just the wrong mix of players,
perhaps an unsuitable replacement ball or simply overall lethargy from dinner—could sometimes combine to
ruin a TFL game.

While the rest of us sat on the *Courier* box in front of
my house and waited for the Robertsons to come racing
down to our end of Tudor some 15 or so houses from
their end of the street, it was always comical, the way
they never came out together but rather, always one at a
time, scattering their entrances like All-Americans being
called through the tunnel over some imaginary loud-
speaker. The last Robertson usually brought the ball,
and held it up triumphantly as he ran.

Too slow to be much of a threat as a receiver, I insisted on playing quarterback, even though I wasn't very good. Through sheer will I became a driving force of TFL, organizing games, lining up guest players to fill in the gaps. My heart was in it; respected veteran Timmy Robertson recognized this and always picked me for his teams, preferring the underdog status my quarterbacking automatically brought. He'd direct the play calling, and sometimes we won on pure emotion, but more often it was his brilliant sliding touchdown catches in our favorite spot, on the grass at the base of the telephone pole in front of Bossy's house.

Eventually, Timmy Robertson and I became "co-commissioners" of TFL, keeping track of stats, records, at times even banning assorted visiting players, like explosive Seneca Street kid Chuckie Long who later swore up and down that Robertson and I only banned him out of fear he would break Bossy's hallowed interception record.

Fall of 1980 was football heaven. I started a scrapbook, showcasing the Monday *Courier-Express* sports pages, clipping out each Bills article. A 3–0, first-place start turned the meanest of nuns at St. Martin's into sweet old ladies. It had people talking playoffs, something to which Bills fans were not accustomed.

The Bills undefeated status in 1980 was especially delicious because as a city we'd taken our fair share of abuse during the prior decade; Buffalonians basked in the notion that maybe, just maybe, people would start to see us in a different light.

Up next were the Oakland Raiders, who'd beaten the Bills in six of the last seven meetings. The Silver and Black may have been in the AFC but to Bills fans they were still somehow in a different league. Winners of the 1977 Super Bowl, regulars on TV, this was a team to be feared.

Villapiano knew the Raiders to the man, having played nine years in Oakland. He wasn't a starter for the Bills, but he took it upon himself to become the team's mental preparation guru leading up to the game, sharing with as many players as would listen his thoughts and insights into his ex-teammates, from observations on their habits and weaknesses to warnings regarding their strengths. Like a man possessed, Villapiano rose up at the players-only meeting on the Friday before the game and began to rant about character and professionalism and about going to war, and when his speech drew to a conclusion chairs and desks were flying around the room. Some of the rookies were dumbfounded by his intensity.

Earlier that week, the city had been rocked by a terrifying killing spree. Four random execution-style murders had taken place, all of the victims black males, all shot with the same .22-caliber weapon. The *Courier*, which dubbed the suspect "the .22-caliber killer," ran chilling black and white police sketches of the suspect for several days on the front page.

That Sunday, the Bills defense terrorized the Raiders, which managed just 37 yards rushing and -13 passing in the first half as the Bills jumped out to a 17–0 lead. Raiders running back Kenny King, who'd lit it up defenses during his first three games, was held to 24 yards on 7 attempts. The Raiders would commit 5 turnovers on the afternoon, two of them fumbles by ex-Oiler quarterback Dan Pastorini. Big Ben Williams hounded the former Oiler all day, sacking him twice, once near the goal line. Jeff Nixon grabbed his league-leading fifth interception.

Meanwhile, the Bills offense, pass-happy a week earlier, switched to a ball control attack, partly on the advocacy of Villapiano, who saw the Raiders secondary as the best cover-crew in the league and the team's strongest suit (indeed the Raiders only points would come on a 48-yard Lester Hayes interception return in the third quarter). The Bills would hold the ball for much of the game, including a 9-minute first quarter drive that featured a dozen rushing plays and ended with a Curtis Brown touchdown sweep. On the sidelines, Villapiano, who would not play a single down, walked the length of the bench, screaming at his teammates not to let up. "Keep attacking!"

When Ferguson did throw, despite the pick returned for a touchdown by Hayes, he was meticulous, 17 for 22, including a 21-yard touchdown pass to Joe Cribbs off a trick play. Knox, decried in Los Angeles for his dull style, seemed to be developing an appetite for risk and a flair for creativity.

Back on opening day against the Dolphins, not only had Knox called an onside kick to start the game, but later in the half, devoid of much offense, he'd ordered up a fake punt that required rookie Greg Cater (in his first NFL game) to throw a pass to rookie tight end Mark Brammer; the play worked and got the crowd into the game.

Now, early in the fourth quarter against the Raiders, the Bills were leading 17–7 and knocking on the door. Knox called for a play he had tucked away on the shelf for about two years. It was a fake reverse, and Fergy executed it flawlessly, flipping a short pass to a wide open

Cribbs who ran untouched for a 21-yard score that made
it 24–7. Cribbs rushed for 90 yards that day. The Bills
gained 235 total yards, but more significant, controlled
possession for an insane 41 minutes.

But still the Bills were denied respect. Even though
the Raiders had been shredded, Lester Hayes, when
asked which team was better, the Bills or the San Diego
Chargers (who'd squeaked by the Raiders in Week 2),
responded by saying the Chargers were "twice as
good." The league would soon find out whether that
was so.

Their 4–0 start was the best since 1975, when the Bills
also went 4–0. Four wins, zero losses. The Bills sat atop
the AFC East; the Dolphins and the Patriots were tied
with 3–1 records. For me, the Bills of 1980 were everything, my singularly favorite aspect of life, and I suppose it was all an escape. When I look back, that season
feels so intensely private, as if the whole experience was
mine and mine alone. My brother Shawn was surely
happy the Bills were winning, but he wasn't obsessed
like I was. He'd rather spend three hours practicing his
slapshot.

It was eerily empty around my house that September,
my dad not there, my mom sick in the hospital. When
my mom finally did come home, she was holed up in
her bedroom for most of the time.

If the Bills 4–0 start was making for a delightful autumn, it was coming on the heels of a summer that I
much rather would have forgotten. In addition to my
parents separating, I'd chunked up—and didn't even realize it. Playing Space Invaders at 7–11 one July afternoon I'd gotten into an argument with a carrot-topped
Timon freshman named Mike Hillary who didn't appre-

ciate my row of ten quarters and my unwavering inten-
tion to play every last one of them. "You're fat you
know," he said. "Fatter than John Milligan." Big Mills
(among the most hardcore Bills fans I have ever known)
wasn't the fattest guy in the neighborhood—the Davis
twins held rank—but I got the picture.

A little earlier that summer of 1980, I'd gotten into my
first of many fistfights on Abbott Road. In St. Martin's
Parish there existed an unspoken order to the way kids
made their way to Abbott Road and its pizza parlors
and corner stores, where we milled about, smoked ciga-
rettes, caused trouble and flirted with the girls in our
class. Like penguins who instinctively know when to
migrate, that summer before seventh grade, my gang of
classmates—Pat Keane, John Fisher, Tommy McDonnell,
Brian George, Moose Moreales, Timmy Gallivan and
Mikey Robertson—took our spot along the designated
chain, in front of Abbot Pizza on the corner of Densmore, which had been vacated by the eighth graders
who now had Anthony's Pizzeria staked out a couple
blocks further down the road. Seventh and eighth
graders hung around Abbott Road, but we weren't
sneaking beers—yet. We'd all end up at Houlihan's bar
soon enough, but for now there was an orderly progres-
sion to teenage drinking. For the most part, it started on
the evening of eighth grade graduation, in Holy Cross
Cemetery. From there, alcohol adventures could expand
to the fields of Lockey's Hill, or behind Public School
No. 67, or in the alley across from Woodside and Abbott.
Timon and Mount Mercy kids went to Caz Park, freshman by the guardrail next to the crick, and beyond that,
within the golf course, different spots were allotted

based on seniority, such as the Yellow Bridge. But it all started in front of Abbott Pizza.

One night, early that summer, our gang crept down Abbott toward the crowd of eighth graders. By encroaching on the Anthony's scene we knew full well we were courting trouble, but that's where the action was, and besides my pal Tommy McDonnell was dating an eighth-grader. We were in the parking lot of Bigelow's Auto Garage when an eighth-grader named Gerry McNamara began flinging pebbles out of a metal tube, strafing me and my friends. I have no idea why I spoke up, perhaps I thought I could take him.

"Quit throwing rocks, asshole!" I yelled.

He asked if I would make him, and before I could answer his sucker punch walloped me in the nose. In a flash of furious humiliation I burst into a hyperactive fit. McNamara covered up. To the group of eighth-graders who hadn't seen the fight's first blow it appeared I was the aggressor. Eighth grader Dougie Engelhardt pulled me off him, and tossed me aside and that's when everyone in the crowd gasped. My nose was badly misshapen. Another eighth grader, Timmy Whelan, looked at me wide-eyed with a ghoulish smile. McNamara yelled out, half apologetically, half tauntingly, "Look, I'll pay for the *fucking* operation!"

But even the Gerry McNamara fight wasn't the worst indignity I would endure that summer going into seventh grade.

End of summer meant final cuts for St. Martin's baseball. It was bad enough that I wasn't even close to being a longshot for the A-team (a few of my classmates had made it), but now it was down to the final cuts for the B-team and still I wasn't yet a solid pick. Making it even worse, my younger brother Shawn was murdering the ball and showing a strong arm from the outfield. I just couldn't hit. On the last day of tryouts, the coach, a really nice guy named Terry Dunford, told us that if he called our names we should come in from the field where we were shagging grounders. That meant you made the team.

There were about 10 of us left out there, and only about four spots. I'm not sure who he called first, but when he called Shawn's name I nearly passed out. Shawn, my younger brother, a sixth-grader, was going to make it and I wasn't. I began to get misty eyed and pulled my cap down as far as it would go, and then Dunford ordered us to bring it in.

"I wish I could have you all on the team," he was saying.

Well, that was it. I was bawling—in front of *everybody*.

"What's a matter?" coach Dunford asked. "Don't worry, you made it."

I knew he was just feeling sorry for me. Everybody knew. Later on, I overheard a classmate, Timmy Michaels, whisper, "Richie only made the team because he cried," but I still felt like I had dodged a bullet.

When you are a little kid, life goes by like one long uninterrupted pleasure cruise. I'd hit my first stretch of rough seas, and the Bills were the perfect escape. I suppose maybe that's how it starts for a lot of people.

Heading into Week 5, the ranks of NFL unbeatens numbered just three: the Bills, the San Diego Chargers and the Detroit Lions. At least one of those teams would stay unbeaten because on Sunday, October 5th the Bills were at Jack Murphy Stadium to face the Chargers and their explosive arsenal. Quarterback Dan Fouts was torching the league, and in spite of how great the Bills were playing, a win against the Chargers on the road seemed like too tall an order.

The Bills took an early 3–0 lead, but the Chargers answered with a 4-yard touchdown pass from Fouts to tight end Kellen Winslow. The Chargers went ahead 14–3 in the second quarter when Fouts threw another touchdown pass, this time to John Jefferson. Trailing 24–12 midway through the third quarter, the Bills still had a chance. They had the ball on the San Diego 10, fourth down and one. But Cribbs was stuffed at the line of scrimmage, and it appeared all hope was abandoned.

I'd been watching in my basement, and stung by the inability of Cribbs to make that first down I gave up and went outside. Some neighborhood kids, a few Robertsons, Skitch, John Gallivan, all of whom had also given up on the Bills, had congregated in front of my house, throwing the football around. The prospect of a good game of TFL football would have been enough to lift all our spirits on a crisp fall afternoon. Plus, the Bills were 4–1, and still in first place, not too bad, I recall telling John Gallivan.

Just then Timmy Gallivan, who all the while had been watching undeterred in his living room, cried out from across the street: "The Bills are coming back! The Bills are coming back!"

We raced over to the Gallivan's house and breathlessly demanded to know what had happened—how was it possible? Timmy did as good a job as he could explaining the turn of events.

It turned out that after the Chargers had held Cribbs on fourth down and took over possession, they had to punt. With 11 minutes to play, Bills backup safety Rod Kush, in for the injured Jeff Nixon, had broken through and tackled the Charger punter before he could get his kick off. A few plays later, Ferguson hit Brammer for a touchdown. Then, on the next series, Haslett had intercepted a Fouts pass and returned it 17 yards to the San Diego 21. That's about the time Timmy had shouted to us.

The replay of Haslett's interception was being shown as we filed in. Mr. Gallivan ordered us to sit down, we were blocking the TV, so we dropped and huddled on the carpet. A few plays later, we all jumped up and danced around as Cribbs, on a pitchout, dashed 3 yards into the end zone for the go-ahead score. With four minutes to play and the Chargers driving to regain the lead, Kush again came up huge, this time with a game-saving fumble recovery at the Bills 25. The Bills hung on to win, 26–24, and all of us kids stormed outside for an evening of street football bliss the likes of which I could never appropriately describe.

Not only had the Bills beaten the highly potent Chargers on the road, but the Lions had been slain by the Atlanta Falcons, which could only mean, impossibly, one thing: The Bills, at 5–0, were sitting alone atop the NFL.

CHAPTER FOUR

TIME TO
TELL 'EM ALL

On Tuesday, February 1, 1977, Buffalo was digging itself out from a devastating snowstorm—more than two dozen people had perished in that awful four-day blizzard, mostly stranded motorists found frozen in buried cars—and on late night TV Johnny Carson was taking digs at Buffalo. Launching into his opening *Tonight Show* monologue over the cheers of his studio audience, Carson wisecracked, "Are you really applauding me or the fact that *you don't live in Buffalo*?"

Watching angrily from his living room in Buffalo was Fred Dentinger, a typically mild-mannered insurance executive whose business writing homeowners policies had been hit hard by the Blizzard of '77. Dentinger had just been named chairman of the Buffalo Area Chamber of Commerce, and he did not take kindly to anyone who made fun of his beloved city. He often told people that he saw the role of chairman of the Chamber as "advocate of Buffalo."

Carson seemed to enjoy making jokes about Buffalo, going all the way back to the early 1970s. Some of these zingers were sent to him pro bono by Alan Zweibel, then an aspiring comedy writer going to school at the

University of Buffalo. The week of the blizzard Carson was as relentless as the storm itself. One joke involved a Buffalo cop standing all day in the snow. Don't feel sorry for me, goes the cop in Carson's quip, feel sorry for the horse underneath me.

Dentinger had no tolerance for what Carson was saying on network television about Buffalo, particularly in light of the fact that the region was suffering a tremendous human and economic hardship. Although it was close to midnight, Dentinger telephoned the Chamber's public relations director, Pat Donlon, sound asleep at the time.

"Damn it all, Pat, can't we do something about this Johnny Carson horseshit?" he asked.

Dentinger demanded that Donlon get him a telephone number for the *Tonight Show* in Los Angeles so he could speak to someone and complain. Still half asleep, Donlon called a contact at Channel 2, the local NBC affiliate in Buffalo. The *Tonight Show* was taped earlier in the day, Donlon's contact explained. Donlon somehow tracked down a phone number of the studio location where Carson's show was taped, even though it was a safe bet no one would be there at that time. Donlon dialed Dentinger back to explain as much.

"I don't care!" Dentinger yelled. "Just give me the number!" He placed the call and berated whomever might have been unfortunate enough to have answered.

Although Dentinger had wanted to take more concrete steps to defend Buffalo's plummeting national image, the reality was that he had bigger fish to fry. Besides having to look after his own insurance interests, citywide his fellow business leaders were already reeling from a declining economy, so the last thing Buffalo needed was widespread damage and lost revenues resulting from a snowstorm. But this had been the storm of the century.

The blizzard dumped six feet of snow on the Buffalo area with some freak drifts as high as thruway overpasses, immobilizing the city for nearly two full weeks. Thousands of people were stranded for days at restaurants, office buildings and schools. A lesser known saga connected to the terrible storm was the raging fire that gutted six homes on the West Side and which for a few tense hours threatened to destroy a huge section of the city. Fire trucks simply could not get through the streets. Had the 50-plus-mph storm winds not shifted when they did, entire neighborhoods might have burned for days. As it was tens of millions in damage and cleanup costs had been inflicted.

Footage from the storm—three-story snowdrifts, pedestrians battered by raging white swirl, completely buried homes—forged Buffalo's image as an urban Antarctica. Forget that Minneapolis-St. Paul is the coldest major city in the lower 48 states (it once reached 41-below in January 1889) or that Syracuse gets a foot-and-a-half more snow than Buffalo on an average annualized basis; the wintry reputation buttressed by the Blizzard of '77 stuck like car exhaust on a pile of snow in the Seneca Mall parking lot.

By the late spring of '77, after our winter of disbelief—all told 199.4 inches of snow had fallen—came to an end, and the last of the Andes-high snow mounds around town had eroded into glass-sharp, blackened muck, the city of Buffalo was still licking its wounds.

When he wasn't trying to find a way to help area businesses cope, Dentinger spent a lot of his energy dealing with internal Chamber politics. He and some of his fellow directors were unhappy with Chamber president Chuck Light, who was the organization's top salaried executive. The Chamber's board of directors, who served as elected volunteers, viewed Light as complacent and ineffective. A group of dissident directors were seeking ways to encourage Light to retire so they could bring aboard a replacement more lock step with their agenda.

Among the issues seen as inadequately addressed by Light were the most basic functions of any Chamber of Commerce—business retention and economic development. Improving the city's image was also part of the mix, but no specific activities were ever seriously undertaken, although as a result of Dentinger, a fuse certainly had been lit.

Dentinger was succeeded as Chamber chairman by his close friend, Frank McGuire, a no-nonsense South Buffalo native born of Irish-immigrant parents. McGuire's Industrial Power and Light was among the better known corporations in the region, and he also owned interests in a range of other businesses, including a few nursing homes and the popular West Seneca nightspot, The Pierce Arrow. In addition to dispensing power via his company, which did electrical contracting primarily on commercial construction projects, McGuire wielded it in Democratic Party politics as an effective fundraiser.

McGuire shared Dentinger's resentment toward Buffalo-bashing and would have forcefully set about to fight back against it. But in late 1978 he resigned as Chamber chairman to run, unsuccessfully, for Erie County Executive, losing the race to a former Bill, Ed Rutkowski, who with the exception of offensive line played just about every position for the team during its AFL heyday.

McGuire was succeeded as Chamber chairman by Andrew B. Craig, III, then president of M&T Bank. In a blue-collar city like Buffalo, the upper crust, white-shoe set are often begrudged, however Andy Craig was hardly of silver spoon upbringing. Born to a hard-working general store owner in the rural town of Jasper, near Bath in Steuben County, Craig was only the second person in his family to attend college, enrolling at Cornell University in 1950. When he graduated, Craig served two years in the Army before landing a job in the big city with M&T. For Craig, that big city was Buffalo. He worked his way up from teller trainee to chief lending officer to president by age 40.

When Craig accepted the post as head of the Chamber in 1979 he had even more national image problems with which to grapple as the world's media descended on the area to cover the Love Canal environmental saga in nearby Niagara Falls. The tragic stories of residents suffering from horrendous ailments linked to toxic waste rising up from below their homes gave way to an inspirational civic uprising of ordinary housewives led by Lois Gibbs, president of the Love Canal Homeowner's Association, who was joined by other neighborhood folks demanding that Hooker Chemical and the federal government own up to the hazardous dumping. But the national media fallout from the environmental debacle mushroomed, and produced yet another black eye for Western New York.

A few years earlier, the smash hit musical "A Chorus Line" opened on Broadway, featuring a dancer named Bobby who utters, "But then I realized to commit suicide in Buffalo would be redundant." ABC-TV sports-caster Howard Cosell once snidely referred to Buffalo as a "clone of Cleveland" during a 1979 *Monday Night Football* broadcast, which wasn't so bad, but then Cleveland Browns coach Sam Rutigliano remarked of Buffalo, "it's not the end of the world, but you can see it from there."

Buffalo Mayor Jimmy Griffin didn't appreciate Cosell's comment. Even though the remark was possibly more insulting to Clevelanders than to Buffalonians, Griffin wasn't naïve; he knew the exaggerated perception of Buffalo being synonymous with urban blight was being perpetuated.

Griffin was a "Give 'Em Hell" Irishman from South Buffalo's old First Ward who'd fought in Korea and worked on the Buffalo Creek Railroad before serving as a city councilman and state senator. He had been determined to become Buffalo's mayor. When he lost the Democratic Primary in September of 1977 to city council member Arthur Eve, Griffin rocked Joe Crangle's Erie County Democratic political machine and switched to the Conservative line. With a solid South Buffalo power base, Griffin then ran successfully against Eve later that fall in the general election. Griffin may have split the Democratic party, but he maintained a tight grip on the city, aided by a cadre of loyal allies, including his brother Tommy Griffin, who became Parks Commissioner, big Stan Buczkowski, a foreman at Republic Steel who served as Griffin's transition team manager, Southside legend Scanoots Scanlon, who ran The Aud, as well as the burly Hennigan brothers, Joe and Bob, revered, and at times controversial, Buffalo cops.

"The people of this community have striven for years to overcome the unfounded negative misconceptions that have developed about Buffalo, and it is extremely frustrating to hear those years of effort mitigated by an off-handed comment before a national television audience," Griffin wrote in a letter to Cosell. "On their behalf, I ask you to show a little more restraint and respect in referring to Buffalo in the future."

Buffalo had been pushed around by the media for too long. At the Chamber of Commerce, Andy Craig decided enough was enough; it was time to push back.

Toward the end of 1979, Craig delivered specific instructions to his new salaried executive, R. David Smith, recently recruited from the Chamber of Commerce in New Haven, Connecticut, to replace Chuck Light. Craig gave Smith a priority: Undertake a program to improve Buffalo's image.

It would not be the first time in Buffalo's history that its leaders had set out to try to forcibly instill civic pride. Of course, for the better part of two centuries there would have been no need for such an effort. Buffalo pride had been around for almost as long as the city.

Established briefly by French pioneers as a short-lived trading settlement in the mid-1700s, Buffalo was not permanently settled until around 1789 when a whiskey-peddling Dutch trader from the Hudson Valley named Cornelius Winney established a trading post near the foot of present-day Main Street downtown, an area at the time known as Buffalo Creek. By the turn of the nineteenth century, Buffalo was a bustling little village. In August of 1810, in possibly the earliest recorded Buffalo bash, then New York State Senator De Witt Clinton, passing through town as part of Erie Canal preparations, lamented in his personal journal, "There are five lawyers and no church in this village."

But with Clinton's mother of all public works projects—the roughly 360-mile Erie Canal, completed in 1825—Buffalo evolved into an economic juggernaut during the industrially transformative era of steamships, giving rise to unprecedented commercial trade on the Great Lakes. In 1900, it was predicted that the "Queen City of the Lakes" would by the next century become the single greatest American metropolis. Scores of manufacturing companies were drawn to Buffalo, with its abundant electrical power, courtesy of Niagara Falls, and bountiful workforce from its large Irish, Polish and Italian communities. In the Census of 1850, Buffalo's population was recorded at 42,261. By 1950 Buffalo counted more than one-half-million people. General Motors and Ford both established major plants in Buffalo. During World War II, Bethlehem Steel in Lackawanna was the largest steelmaking operation in the world, employing 20,000. Buffalo was a global headquarters for flour and grain milling, with major complexes operated by both General Mills and Pillsbury. The tiny Buffalo Creek (pronounced "Crick") Railroad controlled one of the most important three-mile stretches of track in the free world as it hauled tons of Gold Medal baking flour, Wheaties and Cheerios the short distance to other larger railroads. Buffalo's freight railroad terminal was the second-largest in the country, behind only Chicago.

In the Great Depression era of the 1930s, Buffalo began to slowly shed jobs along with the national prominence it enjoyed at the turn of the century. During the late 1930s, local newspapers ran ads proclaiming "Don't Knock Buffalo."

During the 1960s, the completion of the St. Lawrence

Seaway had overnight rocked the Buffalo economy by diverting shipping lanes. Suddenly the Great Lakes freighters that once dropped off Midwestern grain for milling and storage in Buffalo could instead just continue straight through to the Eastern Seaboard and the Atlantic.

Around this time, the Chamber of Commerce sponsored a vaguely conceptualized feel-good initiative called, "Boost Buffalo: It's Good for You." But Buffalo continued to sag. People migrated out of the city, and the tax base further eroded. Between 1950 and 1970, 117,000 people moved away, leaving just over 400,000. Many residents moved to the suburbs, others left the area entirely.

The "Boost Buffalo" campaign was developed by a subcommittee of local advertising agencies. It featured print ads and a catchy radio jingle, all produced gratis by the agencies and carried as a public service by the *Courier-Express* and *Buffalo Evening News* papers, as well as by local radio stations such as WKBW.

But "Boost Buffalo" had no tangible goal, and after a few months it faded away, right around the time Buffalo's national image began to seriously deteriorate in the late 1960s.

In mid-September of 1968, *San Francisco Chronicle* sportswriter Glenn Dickey, then a beat reporter traveling with the Oakland Raiders, formally dubbed Buffalo "the armpit of the East." He'd penned a semi-satirical column taking jabs at the city, and this *after* the Raiders already had lambasted the Bills 48–6 at War Memorial Stadium in Week 2. Even though Buffalo brimmed with architectural landmarks, it was continually depicted as an eyesore. "It's a town that seems to take pride in its ugliness," Dickey wrote. "People here take their football seriously. After all, what else is there?"

A Buffalo native living in the Bay Area saw Dickey's page six column in the *Chronicle* and mailed it back to *The Buffalo Evening News*, which reprinted it a week later on the front page. Not long after that episode, the Chamber started giving visiting writers tours of the city to show the positive aspects of the community.

The following year the national media made much of O.J. Simpson's reluctance to sign with the Bills who had made the USC star and Heisman Trophy winner their number one draft pick. After the Blizzard of '77 hit, evening newscasts around the country led for a solid week with scenes of two-story homes buried in snow. Buffalo had become a national punching bag.

While it didn't go far, the "Boost Buffalo" effort was at least a raw starting point, a touchstone, for the four men who in 1979 would get the ball rolling on what was known as the Buffalo Area Image Campaign. They were: Andy Craig, Dave Smith; Liberty National Bank & Trust Co. president Bob Donough, who was the Chamber board member assigned to oversee the campaign, as well as the Chamber's internal PR man, Pat Donlon.

Donlon was a Canisius College grad and the guy who had been requisitioned with the task of tracking down Johnny Carson in the middle of the night. He'd spent much of his time writing tedious press releases about Chamber luncheons and ribbon cutting ceremonies, so he was up for whatever the assignment entailed.

Their broad stroke effort to address what they saw as a deeply ingrained citywide inferiority complex began to percolate in the summer of '79. From the very start the Chamber leadership uniformly believed that Buffalonians both accepted the knocks against their own hometown, and also unwittingly reinforced them. This line of thinking would not only prove to be out of whack, it nearly set the campaign off on the wrong foot.

Another large obstacle presented itself right away in that the Chamber provided no funding for the area image campaign. Smith and his small staff—essentially Donlon—would need to generate any revenues necessary to cover the costs of the program.

Taking a cue from the Boost Buffalo initiative, which had relied on local advertising executives serving the Chamber on a pro bono basis, Donlon asked Nick Mecca, president of Abbey Mecca & Company, and Woody Smith, vice president of Lloyd Mansfield Advertising, to co-chair a committee of local ad agencies.

Several agencies responded to a letter of invitation, and by the end of 1979 the committee was holding meetings about twice a month. However, problems with this early cooperative approach soon became evident. Not all the agencies attended the meetings on a regular basis, and when they did, too often the representatives were junior staff members, who lacked the authority and knowhow to make important creative decisions. Competitive conflicts emerged, hindering the potential for any kind of consensus. While some agencies were willing to participate pro bono, others insisted upon compensation.

Early in 1980, Donlon made up his mind that the collective approach was not going to work. Not only was it unlikely the Chamber could ever develop a unified campaign, but they couldn't count on the top agencies to do the necessary work on the program. If they couldn't access the top-level creative talent, they couldn't produce top-quality work, and without the latter they could never count on local media to go along with the program.

Donlon informed Smith that the project wasn't working out as well as they had hoped, and that the only way the Chamber was ever going to get anywhere was to make a reasonable investment.

"We have to assume the role of client," Donlon explained, "with a single agency obligated to us."

Smith agreed with him, and the Chamber abandoned the "Ad Council" approach. Dipping into general funds, the Chamber budgeted around $75,000 for the campaign, and began the process that would lead to the hiring of the Healy-Schutte & Comstock Advertising Agency.

It was the winter of 1980, not long after the stirring Olympic gold medal performance of the U.S.A. hockey team helped drag the entire country out of the doldrums, and a 40-year-old advertising executive named Alden Schutte was addressing Chamber members assembled in a rundown office at the old Statler-Hilton.

After a full year of trying to get their image-building project up and running, the Chamber had culled down a long list of local ad agencies to four, Schutte's firm among them. The winner would be given the opportunity to produce the campaign. Schutte was pitching an idea that would lead to something truly special in the history of Buffalo, perhaps the most memorable ad campaign ever produced in Western New York.

A native of North Tonawanda who'd cut his teeth in the ways of national corporate branding as creative director for one of the largest advertising agencies in Chicago for four years, Schutte had questioned the most basic underpinning of the proposed campaign, that Buffalonians held a negative image of their community.

"How can we be sure that Buffalonians don't already feel good about the area?" Schutte asked.

Craig and Donough listened intently. Schutte had given this assignment—a pro bono but high-profile chance to make a name for his firm—a lot of thought. He and his wife, Susan, had friends and relatives from all over Western New York, all of whom loved the area. It was just that they could never quite explain to people from other parts of the country exactly why that was so. Even for those Buffalonians who could express their affinity for the region, sharing the reasons usually proved futile, particularly when confronted with outsiders who automatically pre-assigned the town to winter wasteland status. It was quite possible, Schutte theorized, that one could love Buffalo and at the same time still not know, or for that matter care, how to speak positively about the area when confronted by people from more temperate, "happening" cities.

With his allotted 20 minutes dwindling down, Schutte once again challenged the Chamber board's basic premise, urging them to do the responsible thing—commission a study to find out just how most Buffalonians felt about their hometown before committing money to produce a campaign that might be baseless.

"Let's just be sure your premise is correct," Schutte said.

While the campaign was still in its formative stages, the Chamber made efforts to secure cooperation from the local Buffalo media, which would be crucial if the campaign hoped to have any success. As a result of the high demand, local media provided public-service space and airtime on as equitable a basis as possible, but mostly it was by way of whatever ad slots went unused by paid advertisers. Certainly, the Chamber did not want to see the campaign relegated to Barry Lillis's late-night "Cats Pajamas" or in the *Courier* classifieds. But they weren't yet in a position to demand primetime.

Donlon set out to produce prototypes that could be used in making pitches to media decision-makers. In one of these prototypes, former Buffalo Bills linebacker Harry Jacobs (who played alongside Mike "The Tackle" Stratton on the AFL Champion defenses of '64–65) extolled the virtues of living and working in Buffalo. Jacobs ended the clip by saying, "I'm from Illinois but I love Buffalo." The Jacobs audio was later used for a radio demo.

But these prototype commercials were never to actually be produced. The finished products, local media reps were assured, would be of a far greater professional caliber.

Andy Craig personally met with *The Buffalo Evening News* publisher Henry Urban, a longtime friend of the banker who readily agreed to participate. Dave Smith called on Doug Turner, then an executive editor at the *Courier-Express*. A strong Buffalo champion, Turner was equally enthused about cooperating and was able to see to it that general manager Don Maul was on board. Les Arries, president of Channel 4, was a former Chamber chairman who had kept Donlon on as his personal speechwriter after his term had ended, and because of this close relationship, Arries likewise quickly joined the coalition of the willing. At Channel 7, Phil Beuth, station manager, was a member of the Chamber board and wholeheartedly agreed to participate as well.

Only WGR-TV Channel 2 proved to be a stick in the mud, largely because of management turmoil and a pending sexual-harassment suit against the station manager, but eventually Channel 2 signed on.

Radio played out much the same way. The pacesetters were WBEN, WGR, and WKBW. WBEN shared studios and cooperative arrangements with Channel 4. WGR was associated with Channel 2. Norm Schrutt, station manager at WKBW, was a friend of Donlon's from their days together in the Jaycees. Strongly community-minded, Schrutt also pledged his total support to the area image campaign.

Response from suburban newspapers was generally positive, although some were put off by the fact that the theme centered around Buffalo, but not necessarily their communities.

With full commitment from the media—ultimately $3 million dollars worth of air time and print space would be donated—the Chamber set out to produce the real thing, a civic movement aimed at overcoming the perceived negativity in the Buffalo area.

Of the more than a dozen ad agencies that had responded to the chamber's request for proposals, four finalists were selected: Barber and Drullard; Faller Klenk & Quinlan; Healy-Schutte and Levy King & White. Barber and Drullard prepared a scratch audio tape that concentrated on recreational and cultural offerings, fairly boilerplate material. Faller Klenk & Quinlan wanted to stage a one-day event with people lined up on opposite sides of the Niagara River, demonstrating cross-border unity. Print ads and broadcast commercials would tie into the event before and after. Privately, the Chamber leadership expressed concern about bad weather on the appointed day or, worse, someone falling into the river and drowning. Levy King & White proposed creating commercials to run in out-of-town markets. In return for running those messages, Buffalo-area media would carry similar advertisements from reciprocating markets. The Chamber found it difficult to understand how ads about Buffalo appearing in, say, Chicago, would address Buffalo's supposed complex.

But it was Schutte who insisted upon taking a survey of Buffalo-area residents to validate the Chamber's assessment, and he proposed to do it at his agency's expense, around $10,000. Based upon the results of the marketing study, his agency would then create a campaign to address the relevant issues.

After a long discussion, the selection committee decided in a 3–1 vote that the assignment should go to Healy-Schutte.

Schutte's wife, Susan, also the agency's research director, immediately hired National Marketing Associates/Survey Service of Western New York, a small local company run by a woman named Beatrice Gorbaty, and her daughter, Susan. They conducted telephone surveys of approximately 700 Western New Yorkers asking how they felt about the area and why. By 1980, the city's population had dropped to around 350,000, although tens of thousands of people had relocated to the surrounding annex of Erie County suburbs: Amherst, Clarence, Grand Island, Kenmore and Tonawanda to the north of the city; Cheektowaga, Depew and Lancaster to the east; West Seneca to the southeast, and the Southtowns— Blasdell, East Aurora, Eden, Elma and Orchard Park.

The survey findings surprised even Schutte. As it turned out, an overwhelming *92 percent* of the respondents answered that they really liked the area, but either didn't know how, or didn't feel the need, to express it. The Chamber leadership had misjudged local sentiment after all.

The Schuttes began working on a nuanced campaign based upon the results of the survey. This endeavor wouldn't be about getting people to feel better about Buffalo, but rather, about getting people to outwardly celebrate how positive they *already* felt about the town on the inside. The concept—to tell the rest of the world what Buffalonians knew—quickly took shape, and a working title emerged: "We're Talking Proud."

A former guitarist in some college rock bands, Schutte set about composing the lyrics for a song to be featured in the television and radio commercial he envisioned. He needed a simple song to carry the message that people were proud to be from Buffalo. After a few weeks of mapping out the broad strokes of the campaign, some verses came to him during a flight to San Francisco where he was headed to attend an industry conference.

> *Buffalo's got a spirit*
> *Talking proud, talking proud*
> *Listen up and you'll hear it*
> *Talking proud, talking proud*
> *The good life that we share*
> *With nice people who care*
> *It's time to tell 'em all*
> *We're up and standing tall*

When it came time to produce the song, Schutte called on a production house/recording studio in the northeast section of Indianapolis called Wolftracks. Started up by a charismatic musician named Mike Wolf, this studio was one of many at that time taking advantage of a sharp spike in small market radio and television jingles being manufactured for local airplay all over the country. For an advertising agency in, say, Buffalo, to hire a highly polished group of musicians, engineers and singers in major, heavily unionized music centers such as New York, Chicago, Los Angeles or Nashville to record a 30-second small-market radio spot not only would have been expensive, it would have been difficult to pull off for the mere reason that the top talent normally wouldn't stoop to work on a jingle. So a cottage industry for jingles sprung up in smaller music industry centers, places like San Diego, Dallas and Indianapolis, any of which could have claimed to be the jingle-recording capitals of the world at the time.

A cadre of in-demand Indianapolis musicians and singers became widely known as the *elite* jingle performers and worked with all the big production houses, including Wolftracks. One of these musicians was Doug Benge, a local sessions man who played guitar and piano and worked out arrangements with his lineup of for-hire recording artists, generally an ensemble of two guitarists, a keyboard player, a drummer, a bass player, two trumpeters, two saxophonists and one trombone, as well as a trio of background vocalists. One such vocalist was Teresa Giles, a 27-year-old wedding singer from Lebanon, Indiana, whose mother had sung in a Big Band. Giles herself got started singing professionally in the mid-1970s when she was called in at the eleventh hour to sing backup as a favor to a friend who was recording a country western 45-single for some obscure performer who'd scraped up the money to have it made.

The producer that day hated the guy's song but told Giles she had a wonderful voice and before long, she was one of a half-dozen "first-call" singers.

Schutte had sent the Talking Proud lyrics to Benge, who spent a few days fiddling and tinkering with them and eventually worked out the music. A week later, Schutte flew to Indianapolis to sit in on the final recording session. Giles, with her country twang, sang lead on "the Buffalo song," as Benge referred to it, and she belted out the lyrics as enthusiastically as she could, considering it was one of three jingles she'd record that day. "Talk*ing* Proud," which became *Talkin'* Proud when Giles sang it, had a certain homespun appeal which contributed to the song's bouncy infectiousness. There was nothing special about this Buffalo song to the performers that day; Benge and Giles, who would later marry and then divorce, would collaborate on hundreds upon hundreds of jingles in the early 1980s, and Talking Proud was merely one of them. Neither would ever know just what they had helped to create.

In the summer of 1980, the first round of the Talking Proud television commercials were set to be filmed. While President Carter had the United States boycotting the Moscow Olympic Games over the Soviet Union's invasion of Afghanistan, the Screen Actors Guild was in the midst of a protest of its own, going on strike in New York and L.A.

The SAG strike meant that many new television shows couldn't be taped, delaying production for the upcoming season. It also meant that many actors and actresses were out of work. One young hopeful trying to make it in New York City was Buffalo native Terry Licata, who was just starting to break into soap operas.

That summer, with no work in sight, she left New York City to return to Buffalo.

Licata grew up the only child of Cosmo and Pauline Licata on the West Side of Buffalo, dreaming of becoming a dancer. She took her first dancing lesson at age 3 and throughout her childhood she took singing lessons, piano and ballet. She studied drama at the Studio Arena School and later got a degree in music from Villa Maria College. She was always performing, oftentimes at Mister Anthony's Dinner Theatre. At just five feet tall, Licata was constantly being told she was simply too short to make it as a model or in show business at all for that matter.

In 1979, Licata (along with legendary Channel 7 Eyewitness News anchorman Irv Weinstein) had a tiny part in the James Caan movie "Hide in Plain Sight" which was filmed on location in Buffalo. The movie, Caan's directorial debut, was based on a true story that took place in Buffalo involving Tom Hacklin, a Dunlop Tire plant worker whose ex-wife married a mob informant and ended up in the witness protection program (with the children from her marriage to Hacklin). The factory worker spent eight anguished years searching for those kids, taking his case all the way to the Supreme Court before the government finally relented.

During a cattle call for extras needed in the filming of "Hide in Plain Sight" a casting agent named Bernie Styles noticed Licata and her long red fingernails. "Look me up if you're ever in New York," he told her. A few months later Licata found herself in New York on some auditions and decided to take Styles up on his offer. He didn't remember her at first, but when she showed him her long blood-red nails he made the connection. "If you can get your Screen Actors Guild card by the end of today I have something for you," he told her. Somehow she was able to do it. That same afternoon Styles cast Licata in a role as a background dancer in the acclaimed 1979 Bette Midler movie "The Rose." A small part, but a huge deal for the actress barely into her twenties.

Licata soon moved to New York City, living out of a room at the cramped Barbizon Hotel for Women. She auditioned night and day, and quickly found steady work in the off-Broadway productions of "Hello Dolly" and "Brigadoon." In 1980 Licata landed a small part in Martin Scorcese's "Raging Bull," the story of boxing champ Jake LaMotta. She played in some bit parts on a few soap operas (One Life To Live, The Guiding Light) and some television commercials, trading her dingy hotel room for a hole-in-the-wall apartment in Greenwich Village. Licata was struggling, and the SAG strike wasn't making it any easier.

Back in Buffalo in the summer of 1980, Licata had been working part time as a manager of a disco in the Grand Island Holiday Inn. She began making the rounds of Buffalo advertising agencies seeking appearances in television commercials. One of the agencies she approached was Healy-Schutte.

Susan Schutte met with Licata about a possible photo shoot for a newspaper ad for AM&As, a local department store and a fixture in Buffalo's rapidly declining downtown. Licata didn't get the job—a more "stately woman" had been chosen for this particular fashion spread—but a few weeks later Licata did something that would change her life forever. She sent Susan Schutte a thank-you card. "Keep me in mind," Licata had scrawled.

By this time it was late August and the Schuttes were trying to cast the leading role in the first Talking Proud commercial, which was set for filming later in the month and which would revolve around a pied piper of sorts who led a pack of good-natured folks around the city, marching to a rousing song.

"We need someone with spunk," Susan Schutte told her husband. He agreed with her that after auditioning 50 some odd girls not a one had been the right fit. On the last day before their self-imposed deadline for casting the lead in the commercial, Susan Schutte opened Licata's note and immediately remembered the little brunette with the energetic smile.

She was perfect.

"Wear something bright," Alden Schutte had told her on the phone the night before the shoot. Licata selected from her closet a red two-piece pantsuit that she used to wear with a white blouse while working as a receptionist.

Because she was so petite and the role required her to get people to follow her, Licata thought she needed to do something that could make her character stand out from the pack. She decided to mimic an upbeat, limbo stick marching style she'd remembered from an early 1970s Dr. Pepper commercial. Licata's signature prance around town arching at a 45-degree angle would soon become the talk of Buffalo.

Scenes were shot over two days, September 11–12, across the city, on Elmwood, in Allentown, and in Niagara Square, in front of City Hall. Local people, many of whom were tied into the Chamber, were assembled to create a mixed bag of friendly characters, like this one guy wearing a straw hat, roller-skating along the waterfront.

During the filming of the scene in Niagara Square, office workers are shown fleeing their places of employment to follow Licata around the streets. Many of them were real downtown workers who were on their lunch breaks enjoying the summertime weather when they began to hear the song blasting from the loud speakers. In droves spirited Buffalonians spontaneously joined in the parade of actors while Schutte staffers scurried along after them, trying to get their signatures for the required release waivers.

Looking around at the swelling crowd from atop of the production crew's van, Schutte smiled at his cameraman and tossed a stack of waivers into the air. Later that night he told his wife, "This is going to be a winner."

Besides a battle cry, the Talking Proud campaign was established to give local people the ammunition with which to defend and promote Buffalo when traveling outside the region.

For starters, when it came to medical, education and housing costs, Buffalo's were among the lowest in the country. The city's cultural contributions—the Albright Knox Art Gallery, scores of architectural gems—were heralded. Interesting footnotes tying Buffalo to history, sports and culture were gathered. President Millard Fillmore, for example, was born in Buffalo and had been mayor of the city. The windshield wiper, that hallmark of mankind's progress and ingenuity, was invented by a man from Buffalo. The famous songs "When Irish Eyes are Smiling" and "Over the Rainbow" came courtesy of tunesmiths who hailed from Buffalo as well.

No amount of interesting trivia however could change the cold fact that the recession of 1980 was hurting the city, and furthermore, economic revitalization attempts had not yet created many new jobs. At 11 percent, Buffalo's unemployment rate was among the highest in the state of New York, with layoffs largely impacting steelworkers and autoworkers.

The Talking Proud campaign was formally kicked off on Wednesday, September 24, 1980, with a reception held at the then new waterfront Buffalo Hilton (now the Adam's Mark Hotel). No one knew whether the campaign would take hold. The "sneak preview" event was attended by members of the Chamber, Mayor Griffin, County Executive Rutkowski, Licata, the Schuttes, politicians and other dignitaries, all clapping and singing to the brand new Talking Proud song while an overhead projector splashed the words on a large screen directly behind the wooden podium, itself adorned with the logo, "We're Talking PROUD," an intense-looking cartoon Bison springing forth from the "O." Print layouts, proclaiming "Listen Up America," and depicting a hoard of hardworking folks, a policeman, a nurse, a school teacher, were also unveiled.

As they were leaving the hotel, Chamber president Dave Smith remarked to his PR man Pat Donlon, "Well, a month from now we'll either be heroes or we'll be looking for new jobs."

Two weeks later, at the Chamber's monthly breakfast meeting, about 200 people gathered at the Statler for another major showing of the new campaign. Donlon had gone ahead and ordered 10,000 gold Talking Proud lapel pins, but when Smith found out he'd purchased so many he barked, "We're going to end up eating those!"

By late October, the commercials featuring the feisty brunette in the red suit singing the catchy song began to air practically nonstop in the Buffalo area. Some mocked it outright; the art community and college kids from

Long Island and New Jersey dismissed the commercials as tacky and annoying. One resident wrote *Buffalo Evening News* columnist Bob Curran to ask, "What numbskulls dreamed up that Talking Proud nonsense? If any place has to be ballyhooed, there is something wrong." Meanwhile, area boozehounds coined their own slogan: "Talking Plowed." Many people didn't know what to make of the campaign or simply ignored it.

That was all about to change.

CHAPTER FIVE

RAINY COLTS SUNDAY

When the Bills returned from San Diego at about 2 A.M. on the morning of Monday, October 6, a few thousand fans were waiting in a parking lot adjacent to the Greater Buffalo Airport to greet them. Their 26–24 win over Dan Fouts and the Chargers was astounding for numerous reasons: they had beaten one of the best teams in the league; they'd extinguished, in the clutch, one of the most combustible NFL receiving corps (Charley Joiner, John Jefferson, Kellen Winslow) ever assembled, having overcome a two touchdown deficit late in the fourth quarter, on the road—on the West Coast no less; and on top of all this, the Bills had been penalized only *once* for a grand total of four yards, a team record. Fans were hardly accustomed to such feats. The Bills just did not win on the West Coast. The last time the Bills won a game in the state of California was back on Thanksgiving Day in 1966 when the Jack Kemp-helmed team won in Oakland, 31–10. During the 1970s, if the Bills were flagged once *per series* that could be something to feel positive about.

All the more baffling was that the Bills were 5–0. For the Bills to sprint out of the gate so authoritatively—*five wins and no losses*—was entirely unexpected, and all over town fans instinctively knew it was something to savor.

It was the best Bills start since 1964. Just three years earlier, the Bills began the season 1–5. Now with the mezzanine-level Baltimore Colts coming into Rich Stadium for a game on October 12, there was an excellent chance the Bills would be 6–0 heading down to the Orange Bowl for a rematch with the Dolphins the following Sunday. "The Streak" might have ended, but it didn't change the fact that the Bills hadn't won in Miami since 1966.

The unblemished '80 start raised the theoretical possibility, however outlandish, that it was at least conceivable the Bills could reach the *Super Bowl*. Western New York was decidedly unprepared for such contemplation.

From the blind-faith die-hards to the most hardened pessimists, Bills fans everywhere were suddenly forced to loosen up the chains of their imaginations. The modern Super Bowl and all of its network pageantry was purely exclusive to the rest of the league, like a reserved table at a swank restaurant where only the Dolphins, Steelers, Raiders, Vikings and Cowboys could dine. The Bills weren't only uninvited, they'd long seemed condemned to the soup kitchen.

Unlike today's salary-capped NFL in which a franchise can feasibly go from worst in the league to the Super Bowl in two seasons, the structure of the league during the 1970s allowed dynasties like the Steelers and the Cowboys to flourish, while teams with losing records usually required a minimum of five seasons to right their ship to merely qualify for the playoffs. While there was free agency, compensation requirements

under the so-called "Rozelle Rule" (that the team signing a veteran free agent must provide "fair and equitable compensation" to the team which lost the player)
effectively made free agency meaningless.

Rarely did a team with a losing record one year suddenly come high-stepping into the playoffs the next, although the Tampa Bay Bucs did manage to go from
being the first team in history to lose all of its games in
1976 to the NFC Championship game in 1979.

The Bills turnaround, not unjustly, was credited to the
ex-Ram coaching staff, particularly Knox, as well as his
top lieutenants, defensive coordinator/linebackers
coach Tom Catlin and offensive coordinator/offensive
line coach Ray Prochaska. Catlin, a former All-American
Oklahoma Sooner linebacker who'd helped architect the
great Rams defenses, completely overhauled a Bills defense that just two years ago couldn't halt a rushing attempt if it were being made by a South Buffalo
Shamrock.

But the real catalyst was the fresh lifeblood animating
a team which for many years had been stagnant. Aug-
menting the best Bills talent he'd inherited in 1978,
Knox completely retooled. Leading by example, Dobler
stoked up the offensive line, left for the scrap heap after
the loss of DeLamielleure. Now suddenly the Bills had
the best line in the league. Villapiano, determined to
make the best of his cheerleader role, had instilled in the
defense a kill-or-be-killed, throw-your-body-around
philosophy he'd learned in Oakland. Defensive captain
Shane Nelson, another team leader, was also inspiring
teammates with his intensity on the field. On the other
side of the ball, Joe Ferguson was blossoming into a top-
shelf passer.

Well known in 1980s was the fact that some Bills players (the most bold culprit being Isiah Robertson) were living fast and partying hard, and Knox was either blissfully ignorant or consciously looking the other way. This was a more lawless time for the league, no question. The era of mind-bogglingly monstrous salaries made possible by oversized network television contracts and "Plan B" free agency was still a decade away, while ESPN and 24-hour cable channels were in their nascent stages. The upshot was professional football players weren't as intensely scrutinized, or hounded, by the mass media. At the same time, the country was smack in the middle of a period of surprisingly rampant cocaine usage, not just throughout the pro sports world, but also permeating a large swath of the disco-fueled American social scene. If Knox was playing a game of "don't ask, don't tell," he may very well have been adapting to survive the reality of the times, and a league gone wild.

Either way, the Bills had themselves one kick-ass defense. In five games, the unit allowed just 74 points, fewest in the AFC and third fewest in the entire league behind the Eagles and Cowboys. In three of the first five games, Bills opponents were held to only a single touchdown.

It was a youthful, spirited platoon. At its core was Fred Smerlas, the brutishly lovable 6'3", 280-pound nose tackle around whom a new 3–4 formation had been assembled in 1979. In just his second year, Smerlas had fully arrived as a pro, assuming much of veteran Mike Kadish's playing time. A native of Waltham, Massachusetts, Smerlas traced his lineage to a quasi-mythic figure named George Smerlas, a hairy, seven-footer who supposedly lived in the hills of Greece at the turn of the century and was known to his countrymen as "The Tree." Smerlas was built like a Sequoia. He could have gone to Notre Dame on a wrestling scholarship and there was no shortage of programs—Syracuse, Tulane, USC, Michigan—interested in the enormous high school lineman.

Smerlas, who'd never been out of Waltham, settled on nearby Boston College. By his junior year, NFL scouts were pointing to him as a top prospect. In Smerlas' senior year, B.C. finished 0–11, among the only winless major college programs in the country. Coming out of the 1979 draft, Smerlas looked to be a first round pick, but when the second round began he'd already been passed over by a couple teams, including the Patriots, who were expected to take him. The Bills nearly passed on him in favor of Mark Gastineau, even going as far as to make arrangements to fly Gastineau in from East Central Oklahoma. But at the last minute Knox decided Smerlas, a nose tackle, could make a bigger impact.

In his first NFL game, Smerlas went opposite Steeler Mike Webster, one of the most fearsome centers to ever stand on three points across the nose of an NFL football. Smerlas held his own. Knox didn't like starting rookies, but Smerlas played hard, and there was Kadish, a Hells Angel in pads, to help shoulder the load. Smerlas sat out the last three games of the 1979 season due to a knee injury, and then re-injured his knee during the off-season playing a game of pickup basketball, requiring arthroscopic surgery. To make matters worse he would later suffer a bout with gastritis, spending much of his time at training camp vomiting, dropping nearly twenty pounds. He'd started on opening day against the Dolphins but continued to share time with Kadish, a mainstay starter on the defense line since 1976 who'd switched to nose tackle to help Smerlas usher in Knox's new 3–4. But by Week 2 Smerlas was getting most of the playing time.

Behind Smerlas were arguably the league's best inside linebackers, Jim Haslett and Shane Nelson. Nelson, who grew up near Corpus Christi, Texas and played at Baylor, was passed over by every NFL team in the draft of 1977, but somehow managed to get a tryout with the Cowboys. Every year Dallas would hold a big, pre-camp open tryout in which Tom Landry sifted for one or two diamonds in the rough. Nelson turned out to be one of those lucky Landry finds. The iconic fedora-wearing coach even tried to sign the standout middle linebacker to a two-year contract. However, Baylor coach Cotton Davidson, a former quarterback with the Oakland Raiders in the mid-1960s, had made some calls around the NFL on behalf of Nelson and convinced him to go to Buffalo where he would get a chance to start. "Dallas has Randy White," Davidson told him. "Buffalo doesn't have anybody." Nelson eventually met with Stew Barber, who invited him to a tryout that June and signed him as a free agent. Nelson had his best season in 1979 when he led the Bills with 192 tackles.

Five games into the '80 season it had become apparent to opposing teams that it was nearly impossible to generate any yardage against the Bills on straight-ahead rushing plays. Anything up the gut was stuffed by Smerlas, Haslett and Nelson. Sportswriter Mike Dodd of *The Buffalo Evening News* would dub the trio "the Bermuda Triangle" into which running backs disappeared.

Among the biggest impact players on defense was safety Jeff Nixon, a second-year player who after Week 5 of the 1980 season led the league in interceptions with five. Nixon was the son of a career Air Force officer. He was born in Furtsenfeldbruck, Germany, but his father bounced around a lot—from Cape Cod to Oregon and then to Colorado Springs. Eventually the Nixons went back to Germany, living on a base near Frankfurt where son Jeff played his first game of football in a league organized for the kids of the U.S. servicemen. Later, when Nixon was a teenager, the family moved to Triangle, Virginia near the Quantico Marine base. The family's surname may have been disgraced by the mid-1970s in the wake of Watergate, but by this time Jeffrey was doing the Nixons proud playing defensive back at Garfield High School near Quantico. He was recruited to the University of Richmond where he was first-team All-American, setting school records for career interceptions and return yardage. Nixon (6'3", 190-pounds) had a state trooper's mustache and a boyish grin. As a rookie with the Bills in 1979, he upended the career of one of the best safeties in Bills history, popular Tony Greene.

It was November 18, 1979, Week 12 and the Bills, 5–6, were hosting the Green Bay Packers at Rich Stadium. Midway through the second quarter the Packers took a 9–6 lead on a touchdown play in which James Lofton burned Tony Greene on a 34-yard pass on fourth and short yardage. Nixon, a fourth-round pick who'd seen plenty of action in nickel situations, was a favorite of defensive backfield coach Jim Wagstaff, a former defensive back for the Bills (1960–61) and who was yet another of Knox's Ram imports. Wagstaff was partly responsible for building in Los Angeles one of the best secondaries ever. At half time Wagstaff pulled the rookie aside, telling him, "Nixon you're starting the second half." Greene, second on the Bills all-time interception list behind Butch Byrd, and a two-time All-Pro who was well-liked by players and fans alike—but a step or two slower coming off knee surgery and not known for his run-stop abilities—was benched. With the game tied 12–12 and the Packers marching early in the fourth quarter, Nixon intercepted a pass near the Bills goal line. Ferguson then led the Bills on a 9-minute drive to win the game, 19–12, pulling their record to 6–6. Nixon took over; the following year, Greene was waived.

There's a rookie football card of Jeff Nixon which has a little blurb on the back explaining how the safety is a descendant of composer Johann Sebastian Bach, and while his mother's maiden name happens to be Bach, it merely turned out that some football card fact gatherer had misinterpreted a passing joke made by Nixon. Nevertheless, he was on his way to composing a spectacular year in 1980 when he blew out his knee early in the Week 5 game against the Chargers. During a goal line stand Nixon did his best to stuff the run piling in behind Shane Nelson, who'd tossed aside enormo-Charger lineman Ed White. But unfortunately, White's Volkswagen-sized leg came around and whipsawed Nixon's knee, which caved in 30 degrees the wrong way. As Nixon lay on the field after the play many of his Bills teammates looked the other way, not because they couldn't bear the sight of the awkwardly dangling limb, but rather, because Nixon's blood-curdling screams were making them uncomfortable.

Nixon's replacement was second-year backup safety Rod Kush, who had missed the entire 1979 season with a fractured foot. During the off-season, Kush had helped one of his buddies back home in Nebraska train attack dogs as a way to stay in shape. Donning heavy foam arm pads, he would infuriate German shepherds, running back and forth, over and over, until he'd whipped them into a snarling frenzy. Against the Chargers, Kush came in and played the game of his life, snuffing out two punts and recovering two fumbles, but he *blew out his knee* early in that same game. Since he was the last backup, Kush couldn't come out, thus being forced to play an entire half despite his torn cartilage.

Watching from the stands of Jack Murphy Stadium that day in Week 5 was retired Ram safety Bill Simpson. At 28, Simpson was completely out of football, the victim of his own knee ailments. A few operations and two years removed from his last start, Simpson was contentedly employed as the manager of display advertising for a chain of weekly newspapers in Orange County, California. As he sat in the end zone with his brother Pat, and Betty Anne Cappelletti, wife of ex-Ram John Cappelletti, Simpson didn't think much of it when the Bills lost their two safeties, Nixon and Kush. But after the game, when Simpson stopped by the Bills locker room to say hello to his old coaches, Wagstaff and Catlin pounced on him. "You ready to come back?" Wagstaff asked, though Simpson thought he was just kidding.

Simpson's last game had come 21 months prior. After knee surgery, his fourth in five seasons, Simpson was traded to the Bills, but upon arrival flunked his physical and decided to retire. He had shrugged Wagstaff off. But later, in the middle of the night, the phone rang at his home in Garden Grove, California—it was Wagstaff, who'd just gotten back to Buffalo, pleading, "Come on Billy, I need you."

Simpson certainly knew Catlin's system; he'd played five seasons in L.A. at a time when the Rams had one of the best defenses in NFL history, with Jack Youngblood, Fred Dryer, Merlin Olsen and Hacksaw Reynolds—a squad which in the 1970s recorded the most sacks, and allowed the fewest total yards, fewest rushing yards and fewest total points of any team during the decade.

One notable member of that famous L.A. defense was now a Bill—linebacker Isiah Robertson. While some of his teammates couldn't stand him and second-guessed his abilities, Robertson provided a certain spark. A flamboyant personality who was known to hang out with Rick James in the soul singer's exclusive Eagle Heights home, Robertson was a regular on the Pierce Arrow scene. He was one of the NFL's original bad boys, at times a disruptive locker room presence with a tremendous ego. When Robertson had demanded more money in 1979, the Rams responded by shipping him off to Buffalo. Addicted to the Hollywood lifestyle, Robertson, a native of New Orleans, felt banished and struggled to adapt to life in Western New York.

Around town, the bearded, fur-clad, nightspot-frequenting Robertson was considered a star player, a symbol of the new, more talented Bills. After all, it had been Robertson's game-cementing interception and return against the Dolphins on opening day which had hotwired into place the team's early season momentum.

Buffalo's resurgence under Knox was owed to more than just enthusiastic veteran spirit and improving defense. There had also been plenty of offense, and in particular, a greatly improved passing game.

Ferguson, playing in his eighth year as a Bill, finally had a high-quality receiving corps. During most of the 1970s Ferguson was accustomed to simply handing the ball off to O.J. Simpson, especially late in games, playing conservatively and often timidly. In 1973, the year Simpson ran for 2003 yards, Ferguson averaged just 12 passing attempts per game. Later on in his career, shaky Bills defenses forced him to sit on leads and try to grind out the clock. Points were scored infrequently. It wasn't until 1979 that Ferguson was able to unleash, and in 1980, operating out of the shotgun formation copied from the Cowboys, he evolved into something of a gunslinger. Suddenly, the entire field opened up. The Bills not only had two quality receivers, but they had Cribbs catching passes out of the backfield. Moreover, the Bills for the first time that anyone could remember had themselves a durable tight end with a flair for getting open and reliable hands.

Mark Brammer was a 6'3", 240-pound All-American at Michigan State who had played on Spartan teams with close friend Kirk Gibson. Best known for his gimpy, fist-pumping romp around the bases after hitting one of the most memorable home runs in World Series history in 1988 while playing for the Los Angeles Dodgers, Gibson was said to be among the best receivers to ever play college football. Brammer copied Gibson's powerful, intimidating style. Growing up in Traverse City, Michigan, Brammer was an All-American high school player whose team had to travel at least four hours each way for away games because the town was so far removed. The Kansas City Chiefs had vowed to pick Brammer, at that time Michigan State's third leading receiver in history, but as he sat waiting with his buddies in their East Lansing apartment, the phone never rang.

Years earlier, when Bills scout Dave Smith, a Detroit native, had been an assistant coach for Michigan State, he'd shown an eye for talent in recruiting Joe De-

Lamielleure to come play for the Spartans. Smith once coached the Detroit Wheels in the World Football League before its demise and had joined the Bills staff in 1979. By then he was working as a gym teacher and doing some part-time scouting for the Raiders. He'd called Brammer prior to the draft to say the Bills were interested in him, and sure enough in the third round Knox grabbed Brammer, who at the time only knew one thing about Buffalo—that it was cold, just like Traverse City, which was okay by him.

The Bills starting tight end, Reuben Gant, a number one pick in 1974, was considered a fine physical specimen (6'4", 230) with God-given talents, but prone to a piss-poor attitude and slippery fingers. In 1979, Gant, who owned a Tulsa, Oklahoma-based disco called Reuben Gant's Sports Factory, hauled in a mere 19 receptions. In fairness to Gant, he'd suffered a late-season neck injury. Besides, Knox's system didn't figure tight ends into the passing mix. But in moving to the shotgun, Knox and Stephenson began to change that.

In Week 1 Gant started, but Brammer got himself into the game in an unlikely way. His first NFL catch did not come from Fergy, but rather, it was a pass thrown by another rookie, punter Greg Cater, on a daring fourth down trick play that succeeded, and brought the crowd into the game. The momentum didn't last long because on the very next play Ferguson threw an interception. Gant started in Week 2 against the Jets and had one of his biggest plays as a pro, a 48-yard tight end screen. Knox was using Brammer and Gant interchangeably. Brammer caught a short touchdown pass, his first as a pro, against the Saints, and he'd figured critically into the Week 5 win against the Chargers after Gant went down with a knee injury, catching a touchdown pass late in the game to cut the lead to 24–19. Brammer had taken Gant's starting job and became an integral part of the resurgent Bills offense. However, Gant did eventually return to action and still played a fair amount.

But the Brammer-Gant tight end tandem was nothing compared to Ferguson's dynamite wide-receiver duo. Butler and Lewis were both breakaway threats. Lewis, No. 82, the ex-Steeler, third fiddle to Stallworth and Swann, was a joy to watch in his third year with the Bills. Though Lewis had only 11 catches through the first five games, he enjoyed a two-touchdown game against the Saints. Unassuming in his stride and demeanor, Lewis radiated high caliber and grace.

Undoubtedly the breakout offensive player was rookie Joe Cribbs. He was catching balls coming out of the backfield, giving the Bills another offensive wrinkle. Cribbs wasn't just catching screen passes; often he would sneak behind linebackers and catch over-the-shoulder balls twenty yards downfield in the flats, or outright bombs. Through five games Cribbs led the team in rushing (376 yards), receiving (22 receptions) and scoring with seven touchdowns, making him the leading rusher and scorer in the AFC.

Special teams had also improved. Before modest-sized overachiever Steve Tasker made No. 89 famous with his standout special teams play there was another very similar coverage mercenary who wore that number—little Lou Piccone. A delinquent kid who hung around South Jersey street corners singing doo-wop, Piccone didn't even play organized football until his senior year of high school. Just 5'9", barely 180 pounds, Piccone played running back at West Liberty State in

Wheeling, West Virginia, part of the celebrated NAIA conference. Piccone got his start in the NFL as a scab player for the Jets during the short strike of 1974. He returned to the Jets the following summer during yet another NFL labor dispute that saw players from five teams—the Jets, Redskins, Giants, Lions and Patriots— go on strike for about one month.

Piccone was determined to break into the league. Having almost made the Jets as a walk-on in 1973 (he'd been told he would be offered a contract but inexplicably never was), Piccone played semi-pro ball, first for the Youngstown Hardhats and later for the Bridgeport Jets, part of the Atlantic Coast League where he made $29 bucks a game (after taxes). When he finally did get a contract in 1975, the Jets featured the highest paid player in league history at the time, quarterback Joe Namath, who'd just signed a contract for $400,000 a year. Piccone was the lowest paid player in the league, earning just $12,500. He could back up numerous positions, wide receiver, running back, even in the secondary. Piccone was the kind of player who could make something happen with his sheer tenacity, but he was never appreciated—at least not in New York. By 1977 the Jets were paying him enough so that he could afford to buy a used Corvette. One day in late August the car went missing. While Piccone was sitting around the clubhouse waiting for the police to arrive, Jet coach Walt Michaels pulled him aside and said "Hey Lou, sorry to hear about your car getting stolen. By the way, we just traded you to Buffalo."

That first year with the Bills, Piccone started numerous games and was fourth on the team in catches, behind Bobby Chandler, Bubba Braxton and Gant, but it was special teams where he excelled. Piccone was a heat-seeking projectile on kickoffs, a trained hit man. The little guy with the big heart became a fan favorite in Buffalo while his teammates considered him an unsung, indispensable weapon. His stock had risen considerably during the 1979 season when Butler and Chandler both went down with injuries. That season Piccone caught 33 passes for 556 yards.

The 1980 Buffalo Bills had an abundance of blue-collar types, average Joe's who gave everything they had. This spirit was epitomized by another special teams standout, Chris Keating, a second-year walk-on from the University of Maine. Back on draft day 1979 Keating had thought maybe he'd get drafted in the late rounds, but when he didn't get a call by Day 2, he went to pay a visit to his coach, Jack Bicknell, who later would go on to coach Doug Flutie at Boston College. Keating wasn't quite ready to give up his dream: Was there anything Bicknell could do?

"I'll make some calls," Bicknell told Keating, who grew up the second youngest of seven children in Cohasset, Massachusetts, north of Plymouth. Even when his son was starring at Maine, Keating's dad, the town post master, never thought in a million years his kid would play in the NFL.

Bicknell kept his word and called Norm Pollom later that April and asked if the Bills might be looking for linebackers. The Bills had just drafted Cousineau and Haslett, and had their sights set on trading for Isiah Robertson. But because the team was switching to the 3–4, it turned out that indeed they were. On Bicknell's recommendation, Pollom flew Keating to Buffalo for a special tryout. Pollom handed him a roll of "grays" (standard-issue light work-out gear—gray t-shirt and shorts) and he and Catlin put the 22-year-old through a personal combine. After 45 minutes of mainly agility drills, they told him to shower up and then come meet with them. Keating didn't have great speed—he'd sprinted the 40-yard dash in 4.9 seconds. He didn't have tremendous size either, at 6'2", 223. But he looked like he could hit, and besides, Bicknell didn't put his neck on the line for just anybody.

Keating, still sweating buckets ten minutes after his shower, figured they'd thank him for coming down and send him to the airport. He was stunned when Pollom told him that the Bills were giving him a contract. Keating would come into camp as a free agent; if he made the team, he could expect to make $26,000.

"Is there a signing bonus?" Keating asked.

Pollom smiled.

"No, son, there's no signing bonus."

"Well, I need something," Keating replied. "You have to understand, I paid my own college expenses and I'm living at my fraternity house. Between now and the time camp starts I'm going to have to eat."

"How about $1,000?" Pollom replied, offering to mail him a check.

Keating didn't hesitate. "I'll take it."

All of the pieces were in place in 1980—offense, defense, special teams. The kicking game was resurrected with Mike-Mayer and Cater hitting their strides. The undefeated Bills, the NFL's lone unbeaten team, looked to extend their winning ways against the Baltimore Colts at home in Week 6 before a sellout crowd of 80,020. Two of the first three home games had been sellouts; this for a franchise that had only 21,000 season ticket holders.

The Wednesday prior to the game, ex-Ram Bill Simpson, two years out of football and who just a week earlier had been watching the Bills from the end zone seats of Jack Murphy Stadium, had reported to Buffalo for his first practice. With Jeff Nixon and Rod Kush both on injured reserve for at least a month, newly-acquired Simpson, only in town a few days, would start at free safety.

The city of Buffalo was a mixture of euphoria and tension in the week leading up to the Colts game. On that Friday morning area residents were shocked to learn that for the second straight day a city cab driver had been found murdered. Including the .22-caliber slayings, six black men in total had been killed in Buffalo that fall. In the latter two grisly incidents the victims' hearts had been ripped from their chests. East Side community leaders called on police to investigate what they saw as a racist conspiracy. The same night as one of the killings a cross was burned in front of a home on the East Side, a predominantly black part of town.

On Sunday all eyes were on the Bills, favored to win by a field goal. Buffalo had earned the Colts' respect. But the Bills were facing an improved Colts team led by quarterback Bert Jones, coming off a game in which he'd thrown for three touchdowns and rushed for a fourth in a Week 5 win over the Dolphins.

The game was played on a windy, rain-swept afternoon. Buffalo didn't stop the run as effectively as they had during the first five weeks. Colts' halfback Joe Washington was scratching out first downs left and right. Colts' kicker Steve Mike-Mayer, brother of Nick Mike-Mayer, had just hit a field goal with the wind to make the score 10–0 in the first quarter. The points had been set up when Bills punter Greg Cater shanked one into the wind, allowing the Colts to begin their drive at the Bills 30. It was one of two Cater punts humbled by Rich Stadium gusts in the first quarter.

Still, the Bills cut the lead to 10–9, aided by a nearly 10-minute, 94-yard drive. But the Colts came right back. Bert Jones had marched them all the way down to the Bills 8. He hurled a pass toward wide receiver Roger Carr near the goal line. It was intercepted—by newcomer Bill Simpson.

But it was not to be. Simpson's debut INT was nullified because of a dubious penalty on Lucius Sanford, flagged for an illegal bump on Carr. Instead of a game-changing turnover the Colts had first and goal at the 1. Umpire Pat Harder initially called Bills cornerback Mario Clark for tripping Carr, but then changed his mind and called it on Sanford, but then he wasn't sure. By the time head referee Jim Tunney made the official ruling, it was Sanford for an illegal chuck five yards beyond the line of scrimmage, not Clark for interference. Either way, Colt running back Don McCauley would go in for the score, and the Colts took a 17–9 lead into the locker room.

In the second half the Bills defense stiffened. Late in the game, trailing 17–12, Buffalo drove all the way down to the Colts 39 but Ferguson was intercepted by cornerback Kim Anderson in the end zone. All the Colts needed to do now was run out the clock. Sitting at home listening to Van Miller on the living room stereo on that sad, rainy Colts Sunday, I could only bury my head in the sofa while my brother Tommy quietly worked on a 400,000 piece jigsaw puzzle with the patience of a Tibetan monk. Even though the Bills would still be 5–1, hearing Miller explain that the Colts could just take a knee felt like one to the balls. The bursting of the Bills bubble left a pin prick in my heart that to this day whistles with a unique brand of sting each time I bring myself back to that game.

The Bills showed some weakness, shocking us all back to reality. All during the 5–0 stretch the defense had stopped opposing running backs cold (teams averaged just 83 yards per game), but the Colts were able to rush for 142 yards. Ten penalties also hurt the Bills. In addition, the Bills pass rush was unable to register a sack on Bert Jones.

The following week, October 19, 1980, the Bills played the Dolphins in Miami—where they had not won since 1966. Talk about a streak. In 1968 the Bills squeaked out a 14–14 tie against the Dolphins in the Orange Bowl, a game which required the Bills to play four different quarterbacks, possibly a record. Maybe it was the weather, all that distracting sunshine, but during the 1970s the Dolphins outscored the Bills at home 320–157. (It would not be until Week 6 of 1983 that the Bills would finally win in the Orange Bowl, a 38–35 overtime game which marked the first ever start for a rookie out of Pittsburgh named Dan Marino.)

Three minutes into the 1980 Orange Bowl meeting Cribbs got smacked by Vern Den Herder and fumbled the ball, promptly scooped up by Don Bessillieu who ran 44 yards for the touchdown. All of the Dolphins points came off three Cribbs' cough-ups. The ball-control Bills would only rush for 68 yards, a season low. Third-string quarterback David Woodley, in his first start, made the Bills secondary look shoddy, scrambling and hitting timely passes. The unheralded Terry Robiskie piled up 84 yards on the ground.

Late in the game, the Bills desperately scurried to fight their way back. Ferguson led them on a 66-yard drive that culminated with a touchdown pass to Butler with 1:19 left, cutting the lead to 17–14, but the subsequent onside kick was unsuccessful. They'd lost a tight contest for the second straight week.

That already depressing afternoon, I'd received a strange phone call from my best friend Pat Keane's mom. She was sending Pat's older brother Neil over in his car to come pick me up. I was to accept the ride and come straight over to the Keane house on Potter Road near Caz Park. Pat was in the front seat but as we completed the three-minute drive we were not to speak. The whole strange encounter coupled with his terrified expression had me perplexed. I squinted him a "what's happening here?" grimace and he mouthed two words.

The note.

On Friday at school I'd written him in a mix of black and red ink an entire notebook page of scribblings and sketches so profanity-filled, so egregiously filthy in its descriptions of various classmates that surely it would appall any decent person (even today), but at the same time I felt it to be such a creative masterpiece that I'd brazenly initialed it, *RB*. My attempt at Friday afternoon hilarity had ended up being saved for posterity alright, tucked away neatly in Pat's back pocket. On Sunday, Mrs. Keane, a traditional-minded Irish Catholic, had found it while doing the laundry.

"Did you write this?" she asked me point blank.

Her expression begged me to deny it. Looking back I should have, but I choked.

"Yeah, I wrote it."

The consequences were this: Pat and I were to not

hang around together anymore, at least for the time being, and my father was going to be presented with my handiwork. I was totally mortified because the Keanes were like family.

At 5–2 the Bills were now in second place behind the New England Patriots in the AFC East and worse than that, I was in some deep shit. The fall of 1980 had seemed too good to be true.

Suddenly it all was.

CHAPTER SIX

LEARNING TO WIN

Huddled on the sidelines of gloomy Shea Stadium, Joe Ferguson and Chuck Knox weighed their options. Ferguson had used up the Bills final timeout with 12 seconds remaining in a Week 10 battle with the New York Jets, the score tied 24–24. Mark Brammer had just hauled in a 16-yard pass to put the ball on the Jets 31-yard-line.

"Let's go ahead and kick the field goal," Knox said in talking it over in the rain with Ferguson and his offensive brain trust of Ray Prochaska and Kay Stephenson.

Ferguson was inclined to agree, but then again the field was a soggy mess. Plus Mike-Mayer had missed a 44-yarder earlier in the game. The veteran quarterback calmly offered a second opinion.

"Why not try to get 10 more yards?"

Knox thought for a moment and issued Ferguson his marching orders: "Okay, we're going to take one shot at the end zone, see what happens. Maybe we'll get an interference call. If you don't have anybody open, throw it into the stands."

It had been raining on and off all morning that day in Flushing, Queens. Most of the first quarter had been

played in a monsoon. As the cold, damp offense ambled
into the huddle the skies were getting dark. Ferguson,
his white jersey a spotless testament to the best offensive line in football, knew exactly what he was going to
do. He called a play in which Frank Lewis would fake a
15-yard sideline pattern and then make a break for the
end zone. The play had been run all week in practice
and Lewis knew it was coming.

Fergy, standing in the shotgun, could barely contain
himself when he looked to his right and saw that
second-year Jets cornerback Donald Dykes was playing
Lewis in man coverage. With plenty of protection (New
York's world-class lineman Joe Klecko had gotten
nowhere on offensive tackle Joe Devlin all day) Lewis
juked and then broke outside. Dykes took the bait and
there was no one playing Lewis deep. Ferguson, standing patiently back at about the Jets 42, saw he had No.
82 to himself and made the perfect throw. The ball sailed
through the misty, fleeting light of the late afternoon
and dropped in over Lewis' right shoulder. But just then
Lewis stutterstepped, and juggled the ball. Dykes
looked over and hoped to God Lewis dropped it. The
ball bounced up off his hands and spun end over end
right in front of his face. Lewis clasped his hands forward but appeared to lose his grip.

A week earlier at Rich Stadium the Bills had jumped
out to a 14–0 lead late in the first half against the Atlanta
Falcons only to wind up losing 30–14, their third loss in
four games. Suddenly the team that was the talk of the
league was in trouble. Now, against the Jets, the Bills
had blown a 17–0 lead. They had actually been ahead
24–10 midway through the third quarter, but Jets quarterback Richard Todd had battled back with impressive

drives. To make matters worse, Bills cornerback Mario Clark seemingly had the game sealed when he intercepted a Todd pass and returned it 21 yards for a touchdown. But it was called back because of a facemask penalty on Ben Williams. Now the winning touchdown to the wide-open Lewis was about to slip away. If the Bills wound up losing this one they'd be 6–4 after starting 5–0. Maybe it was true, that you really couldn't teach an old dog new tricks.

But just when it looked like the ball was going to splash to the turf, Lewis managed to get a grip. Clutching it dearly, he raced the last few yards into the end zone, unscathed. With six seconds to play, the Bills had struck a fatal blow. Brammer jumped on Lewis. Then Butler and Lewis embraced in the end zone. Next Curtis Brown gave Lewis a bear hug and then Devlin, and soon the entire offense mobbed him. Later, as the Bills were trotting off the field, a pair of diehard Bills fans were down in the front row clapping and yelling at Fergy, who was holding his helmet as he walked into the locker room. Fergy somewhat hesitantly thrust his headgear up into the air over his head, a humble nod to his legion of two on foreign soil.

After the game Fergy told a reporter, "We've been losers for a long time. We're just learning to win."

The local rumor about Ferguson for years was that he mailed it in once hunting season began in the late autumn; he, being an avid outdoorsman, and the Bills season usually being a bust by then. However, nothing suggests there is any truth to this theory.

Although loved as a blue-collar workingman's quarterback, "one of us," Ferguson was just as often knocked by fans for what they perceived in him as a defeatist attitude. But the truth was, he hated to lose worse than anyone; he hated making mistakes.

Before coming to Buffalo, Ferguson had always been a winner. Raised the only son of a house painter in Shreveport, Louisiana, Ferguson excelled in track and field (shot put) and he also sparkled on the basketball court. But Joe Ferguson was born to play quarterback. A jock's jock who grew up a few classes behind another Shreveport throwing legend, Terry Bradshaw, Fergy led his high school football team to the state championship during his senior year in 1968. He was recruited by Frank Broyles to play at Arkansas, one of only a dozen or so college programs in the nation that really liked to throw the ball. All-American as a Razorback, Fergy was named MVP of the Southwest Conference his junior year. Drafted by the Bills in the third round (behind two first-round picks, Paul Seymour and DeLamielleure, and a second-round pick, USC defensive tackle Jeff Winans), Ferguson was supposed to play his first year behind Dennis Shaw. But by the time the newly built Rich Stadium officially opened in August of 1973 for pre-season, Coach Lou Saban had named Ferguson his starter.

On opening day against the Pats at Schaefer Stadium in his first pro game, Ferguson was dropping back for just his third pass when he was sacked so violently he was knocked out. Shaw came in and steered the Bills to a 31–13 rout. But the star that day was O.J. Simpson who, in his fourth season as a Bill, ran for 250 yards, setting an NFL single-game rushing record. Fergy started again on the road in Week 2 against the Chargers, but after going 5 for 12 with one pick, Fergy was benched. Shaw came in again but wasn't much better and the Bills wound up losing 34–7. In Week 3—the first regular season game ever played at Rich Stadium—Fergy led the Bills to a 9–7 win over the Jets. Though he spent most of the day handing off to Simpson, who ran for 123 yards, Ferguson showed poise and control in the huddle in completing his first full professional football game.

Ferguson spent the '73 season handing off to Simpson, who became the first running back to break the 2,000 yard barrier that December. The historic run came on a blustery day in a 34–14 win against the Jets at Shea, a game in which Fergy threw a mere five passes. Few remember that the Bills, who finished that year 9–5, just missed making the playoffs as a wildcard entrant that final Sunday because the Steelers also won, beating the 49ers, 37–14, to push their record to 10–4. Still, Simpson's milestone was one for the ages. It was Fergy who came into the huddle with seven minutes to play in the game, the Bills leading 21–7, and informed his teammates that Simpson—who earlier in the first half had surpassed Jim Brown's single-season mark of 1,863 and then unceremoniously fumbled on the next play—was just 60 yards away from two grand. It was Ferguson who hollered the signals, a play called #27, O.J.'s favorite play, in which Ferguson faked to the fullback Jim Braxton up the middle and Reggie McKenzie charged into the hole.

The next year, the Bills, in possession of the greatest football talent in the land, opened their season on *Monday Night Football*, but this time it was Ferguson who was the star. He tossed two touchdown passes in the final two minutes to rally the Bills over the Raiders, 21–20. Simpson had sprained his ankle and sat out the first half. Fergy was solid in just his second year and by

Week 6 the Bills were tied for first place in the AFC East at 5–1. The Bills finished 9–5, but this time it was good enough for a wildcard spot. It's somewhat remarkable that nine wins would have sufficed. At the time, the NFL did not yet have a second wildcard spot, added in 1978. Regardless, the Bills suffered a lopsided loss to the Steelers in the divisional playoff.

Fergy's third year, 1975, was supposed to be a break-out year. They opened 4–0. In Week 4, a win over the Colts, Fergy had his highest passing yardage day as a pro, throwing for 253 yards. But the Bills ended up going 8–6 and missing the playoffs. Ferguson's three-year contract was up, and during the off-season the Bills traded his star receiver, Ahmad Rashad. Ferguson was exasperated and expressed reservations about returning to Buffalo. But he did. Ferguson broke four vertebrae in his lower back in the seventh week of the 1976 season and was out for the rest of the year. He'd also broken a record by throwing just one interception that season. Ferguson's replacement, Gary Marangi, would throw 16 interceptions in 82 attempts, or about once every five passes. Marangi's backup was Sam Wyche, signed following Ferguson's injury. The Bills, undermined by their poor defense, fell into the NFL basement.

Professionally, Ferguson was miserable. Not only was all of the losing taking a toll, but there was also the parade of great players streaming out of Buffalo. Heading into the 1978 season, Knox's first as coach of the Bills, Ferguson was one of the last Bills left from the Simpson era. Off the field, Fergy, then 28, managed to enjoy himself. Although he was considered one the league's most eligible bachelors, Ferguson was hardly what you would call a night owl. While he only earned a little more $100,000 a year, Ferguson had bought a piece of a fast food burger joint in Monroe, Louisiana called Gabby's. He also splurged for a four-seat, single-engine Cessna, which the experienced pilot flew to go on hunting and fishing trips in Arkansas.

Under Knox, Ferguson's arm was showcased in much the same way that O.J. Simpson's legs had been by Lou Saban.

In 1979, Ferguson threw 458 times, a Bills franchise record, and he became not only the first Bills quarterback to pass for more than 3,000 yards in one season, but also the first Bills quarterback to throw for more than 300 yards four times in a season. He also set Bills records for the most passing yards in a season (3,572), the most touchdown passes in one game (5), as well as the most completions in a game (27).

Prior to the start of camp in 1980 Knox had made the switch to the shotgun in obvious passing situations. The coaching staff kept busy during the off-season, pouring over statistical trends, analyzing film, consulting with one another on ways to improve. Back then, the Bills used to collaborate with the Cowboys, 49ers and Seahawks for a four-team combine, scouting college talent. During one of these combines in Seattle, Stephenson found himself chatting with Cowboys assistant Dan Reeves about the shotgun formation. At the time, the Cowboys were the only NFL team committed to the drop back formation in third and obvious passing situations. Today, the shotgun on third-and-long is about as routine as the fourth-down punt, but conventional wisdom in 1980 held that the shotgun put the center at too much of a disadvantage when coming up to block the opposing linemen, and that the risks of an inaccurate long snap outweighed any rewards. Knox and Stephenson realized it was an edge, a way to put five eligible receivers up near the line of scrimmage in third down passing situations. When the quarterback is directly under center, at least one of the running backs has to stay in and block. Not so with the shotgun. On top of that, the extra time gave the quarterback a better chance to spot blitzing safeties.

Initially, Ferguson couldn't stand the new formation, mostly because he didn't like taking his eyes off the defense even for the split second it took to haul in the long snap, but eventually he grew to enjoy the extra time in the pocket. Never a scrambler, Ferguson was, however, a terrific passer. With Cribbs in the backfield in 1980, the Bills for the first time in Ferguson's career had a passing game and a running game.

More significantly, the Bills finally had a defense—the No. 1 defense in the league.

That stingy Bills defense was on prominent display in Week 11 against the Cincinnati Bengals in front of 41,000 at Riverfront Stadium. The game plan, as usual, was to establish a physical tempo with some hard hits on defense. Cornerback Charlie Romes took the initiative and nearly knocked receiver Don Bass into the Ohio River on a slant pattern to nowhere. Bass left the game with a wounded knee. Cincinnati quarterback Ken Anderson was knocked out of the game shortly before half time, clobbered by Sherman White, in one of four Bills sacks of the day. Outside linebacker Lucius Sanford had one, blindsiding Anderson's backup, Jack Thompson, and forcing a fumble recovered by Bills cornerback Mario Clark.

The play of the defense more than made up for the

Bills offensive struggles. The Bengals had just nine first downs. The only time the Bengals threatened to score all day came in the second quarter on a Cribbs fumble deep in Bills territory, but Romes picked off an Anderson pass in the end zone.

Leading 7–0, the Bills took over at their own 21 after a Bengals punt ended the third quarter. The clock read 14:54. Eighteen plays later, Roland Hooks, escorted by Reggie McKenzie, who took out two Bengals with one furious shove, scored a touchdown on a five-yard sweep. Incredibly, after Mike-Mayer's extra point, just 2:55 remained in the game. The Bills won, 14–0.

The flight back to Buffalo was jubilant. It was a true team victory. The 12-minute drive to ice the game was the longest Knox could ever recall. Just as rare was pitching a shutout on the road. Better still, the Patriots had lost at home to the Rams. The players cracked open beers and guzzled them the whole way home from Ohio, literally riding high.

At 8–3, the Bills were back in first place with five weeks remaining and one of the biggest games of the season just around the corner.

CHAPTER SEVEN

BRING ON THE STEELERS

O n the Tuesday evening following Buffalo's November 16 shutout of the Bengals, linebackers Jim Haslett and Isiah Robertson stood before West Seneca Town Judge Richard Scott to answer to charges of disorderly conduct. Most of the other night court attendees on hand to face moving violations or zoning infractions were quite surprised to see the two star players. Even the judge couldn't help being a little giddy, considering he was a Bills fan himself.

Haslett, then 24, and Robertson, 31, were facing misdemeanor charges following a fight the prior Sunday night at Frank McGuire's Pierce Arrow Restaurant and Night Club on Seneca Street. It should be noted that what went on at the Pierce Arrow during the early 1980s, taken within the context of the times, could perhaps fill another book, although most of the people who were there find they either don't remember much or have chosen not to. But the Haslett/Robertson brawl has become legend.

Following their flight back to Buffalo from Cincinnati, many of the Bills headed straight to the Arrow for more post-game partying. No question, in a city loaded with bars, the Arrow was the place to be. The "Chip Strip" had not yet been born. Back in 1980 the stretch of Chippewa Street between Delaware and Pearl was 700 feet of filth that cast an ugly shadow on all of downtown, and with bars you wouldn't want to go to—such as the notorious Fisherman's Wharf on the corner of Franklin with its long track record of stabbings and prostitution. If a hooker and a fish fry wasn't your idea of a night on the town, you could try the surly House of Quinn, an old man's gin mill that corroded into a topless go-go bar where pimps, thieves and drug dealers consorted and plied their crafts.

The Arrow was located miles from downtown, just beyond the border of South Buffalo, where the hard luck, scruffy world of the Irish Seneca Street "Rats" ended and the more sanitized world of West Seneca Camaros and clogs began. Not only did the players go there to celebrate after games, but they held a Monday night card game there, downing their collective weight in pitchers and shots by the hundred whilst playing endless hands of Boo-Ray and Tonk, and yelling at Howard Cosell, who refused to show the Bills on half-time highlights of *Monday Night Football*. McGuire put out free chicken wings, but crowds gathered for the Bills, not the blue cheese.

Accounts of just what triggered the Haslett/Robertson fight vary, but suffice it to say that Robertson's penchant for instigation and Haslett's famously short fuse collided that night shortly before 2 A.M. Some at the bar reported that Robertson had been sounding off about how much more money he made than Haslett (at $200,000 a year, probably twice as much). Haslett at one point had supposedly called out Robertson for not carrying his load on the field. An alternate version had Robertson picking a fight with backup defensive lineman Scott Hutchinson, and Haslett, fed up with Robertson, intervening. Robertson always maintained that he'd been minding his own business at a table, discussing the Bengals game with Frank Lewis and Sherman White, when Haslett came over and started messing with *him*.

Either way, at some point Robertson got in Haslett's face and the wild kid from Pittsburgh popped him. More punches flew, and in the melee Robertson chomped down on Haslett's ring finger and wouldn't let go. He might have bitten it off had Haslett not been wearing a college ring. With bouncers shoving Haslett and Robertson out the door, the brawl spilled out into the street. Just then West Seneca policeman Jim O'Connor, cruising along in a squad car through the Pierce Arrow parking lot, saw the two players being tossed out of the bar and a crowd gathering around them. He called for backup. Six officers in four cars responded within minutes. It took all seven officers to break it up. Robertson was spitting venom at the police who were cuffing him while somehow Smerlas had managed to convince the officers that he and Haslett were cool-headed enough to call it a night and avoid any further trouble. Just when the police had agreed to let them go, Haslett ran across the parking lot and sucker-punched Robertson, still handcuffed at the time. The cops had no choice then but to haul Haslett and Robertson away.

Knox had gotten a phone call in the middle of the night and was far from pleased the next day at Monday film meetings. He told the team in a stern but subtle way to dial it down. "We got the Steelers coming in here for one of the biggest games of the year," Knox said. "Let's concentrate on taking care of business."

In court Tuesday night Judge Scott had an important question for the two Bills linebackers, who stood before him stone-faced, contrite.

"Do you really think you've got a shot at beating the Steelers?"

"We'll do it," Haslett tersely assured the judge, who then let both of them off with a warning.

Beat the Steelers? Winners of the Super Bowl, their second straight championship and fourth in six years, the Steelers were a tall order even for the resurgent Bills. But the upcoming game had taken on an even more heightened sense of importance, all because of a promotional effort that had come back to haunt the front office.

The Bills ticket manager at the time was Jim Cipriano, an ex-Marine from Youngstown, Ohio. No one could have blamed him for trying to fill the seats back in the spring when the Bills organization was struggling to drum up interest for the season ahead. Selling tickets was Cipriano's lifework. He'd sold them for the Baltimore & Ohio Railroad following World War II, and later for the Pennsylvania Railroad. He'd been the Bills ticket director since 1969. Before that he handled tickets for sporting events at the University of Pittsburgh. Through his connections in the Iron City sports world, Cipriano had arranged for a special promotion with the Steelers organization. A flyer was sent to all the Steelers' season ticket holders, as well as those Steelers fans who'd purchased tickets to the 1978 Bills-Steelers game at Rich Stadium, offering them a special deal on the upcoming November 23rd game. Clearly, Cipriano had underestimated the response and failed to grasp the breadth of Steeler country, which stretched across all of Western Pennsylvania—Johnstown, Lancaster, Harrisburg— even as far as Elmira, New York and Jamestown, which some would assume to be Bills territory. Many of these Steelers fans in the hinterlands could never get a ticket to Three Rivers Stadium, which held under 50,000. When it was all said and done, Cipriano's promotion created an unusual situation for a professional sporting event: Nearly half of the 80,000 tickets for the showdown between the Bills and the Steelers had wound up in the hands of fans of the *visiting* team.

Courier columnist Phil Ranallo compared the move to President Carter selling nuclear weapons to the Ayatollah. An estimated 35,000 Steelers fans stormed into Buffalo that weekend, rolling up the New York State Thruway in RVs and by busloads, many of them feeling superior to Buffalonians, what with the Steelers being among the greatest football teams ever created. Since 1972 only one Steelers team (1977) lost more than four regular season games. The 1980 Steelers were heading into Week 12 with a 7–4 record, and they'd won their last three games.

The Bills, at 8–3, came into the game with the No. 1 defense in the league in terms of total yardage allowed, 2,824, a full 100 yards less than the second-ranked Philadelphia Eagles defense. The Bills, led by the Bermuda Triangle of Smerlas, Haslett and Nelson, were holding opponents to around 100 yards rushing per game.

The Steelers had a pretty good defense of their own, featuring Mean Joe Greene and Jack Lambert. The reigning Super Bowl champs were installed by Jimmy the Greek as 3-point favorites.

The Steelers fans had brought with them enough "Terrible Towels" to clean up a Hooker Chemical spill, but Buffalo had its own secret weapon to stir the crowd, as if a stadium half-filled with enemy fans wasn't sufficient enough.

All year long, Andy Craig at the Chamber of Commerce had been pushing his in-house PR man Pat Donlon to get the "Talking Proud" song played at Bills and Sabres games. However, the Sabres organization wouldn't go for it and Bills public relations director Budd Thalman flatly ignored Donlon's repeated requests as he dealt with a harried scheduled of visiting media, player interview requests and controlling access to the locker room. Finally, a few days before the Steelers game—and some two months after the "We're Talking Proud" campaign had officially been unveiled—Thalman told the persistent Donlon to talk to Mike Shaw, assistant director of public relations. This was good.

Shaw and Donlon had traveled in the same circles throughout the years. When Donlon was doing PR for Canisius College, Shaw, a graduate of St. Bonaventure University, was doing PR for Niagara University, and so they attended many of the same "Little Three" functions. When Shaw was PR director for the NBA Buffalo Braves during their last four seasons (1974–78), he'd secured Donlon tickets on occasion. As deputy Bills PR man under Budd Thalman, Shaw helped facilitate reporters' requests, scheduled player appearances, and then on game day he oversaw the crew that ran the scoreboard. Shaw, after discussing it with Thalman, agreed to play the Talking Proud song during the Steelers game, at the end of both the first and third quarters. Donlon was pleased. He came by Rich

Stadium that Friday and gave his friend an audio cassette tape with a recording of the 30-second song, followed by a brief spoken message, and then another cut of the song.

On Saturday morning, one day before the Steelers game, the Bills players were going through a final, light workout. Shaw was up in the press box checking over the script for the next day's game, which included public service announcements, crowd teasers, and obligatory nods to the various special groups, clubs, and youth organizations expected to be in attendance. He asked the scoreboard operators, stationed in a small booth at the far west end of the press box, to play Donlon's tape to make sure the audio could be heard clearly over the public address system.

Down on the field some of the players heard the song and vaguely recognized it from the commercials. Others wondered aloud why it was being played. Later in the locker room a few players asked Shaw about the song. He had a funny feeling.

The next day, Sunday, November 23rd, in front of the third largest crowd in Rich Stadium history, one of the most eagerly anticipated sporting events in recent memory began to unfold. The Bills took the field and immediately fell flat on their face.

Joe Ferguson's second pass was intercepted by Steeler linebacker Robin Cole, who returned it to the 2. Immortal running back Franco Harris scored easily from there, and before many of the visiting Steelers faithful had even figured out that Rich Stadium was not in downtown Buffalo, the Steelers were leading 7–0.

But Fergy shrugged off the early pick and later in the first quarter connected with ex-Steeler Frank Lewis for

29 yards down to the Pittsburgh 29. Then Fergy aired one out to Jerry Butler, who made a ridiculous catch on the underthrown ball going up, and reaching back over All-Pro cornerback Mel Blount to haul it in. As Butler flew over the goal line for the score, Mike Shaw, up in the press box, figured it was as good a time as any to cue the Chamber of Commerce Talking Proud song. He phoned the scoreboard operators in their booth, along with public address man Danny Neaverth, and told them to play the song. And just like that, history was made.

Still celebrating the Butler touchdown, the crowd quickly recognized the song from the commercials which had run seemingly endlessly all autumn long, and entire sections excitedly began to jig and stomp, swaying and singing along to the words blaring from the stadium's PA system.

"Buffalo's got spirit, talking proud, talking proud . . ."

The Steeler fans weren't impressed; this game was merely tied. But intuitive Bills fans knew that the tide had turned.

Midway through the third period, with the Bills leading 14–10 (Butler victimized Blount for another touchdown catch later in the first half), it appeared that the Steelers might try to scratch their way back into it. The Bills had just seen a 79-yard Curtis Brown screen pass down to the Steelers 6 called back because of a personal foul on Conrad Dobler. Now the Bills were backed up. On third down and 14, as Ferguson dropped back to pass, the Steelers contingent became downright bombastic, sniffing the distinct odor of field position and momentum.

Frank Lewis had left the game with a back injury. His replacement was Ron Jessie, a veteran Ram, and yet another import lured to Buffalo by Knox and his crew. Ferguson hit Jessie for 17 yards and the first down. A few plays later Brown, still a bit winded from his nullified sprint, struck again, breaking a sweep for 34 yards and the touchdown, no flags. It was as solid a run as anything O.J. Simpson had ever turned in. For one thing, it was well established in the league that no one successfully got outside on the Steelers; they were too fast, too well-endowed at outside linebacker. But key blocks from Joe Cribbs and Butler had cleared the way for Brown, who shrugged off linebacker Loren Toews and raced past safety Mike Wagner, and with ten yards to go cut inside, leaving cornerback Ron Johnson in his wake.

The Bills now led 21–10 and Steelers fans could do little but sit silently and listen to the twangy Talking Proud tune play one more time to the delight of the 45,000 Bills backers. Seeing the fan reaction and realizing the song was giving the Bills momentum, Shaw continued to play it any chance he could.

The Bills went on to roll past the Steelers, 28–13, the Talking Proud song playing after each touchdown, and after key plays, so many times that Steeler fans were probably ready to vomit into their terrible towels (either that or start to sing along). In between recordings of the song was a short spoken message from the Chamber of Commerce, but no one could hear it over the roar of the crowd. And Bills fans had plenty to roar about. The Bills crushed the Steelers, held to 239 yards. Meanwhile, the Bills racked up 379 yards. Joe Ferguson, who had spent his entire life in the shadow of Shreveport hero Terry Bradshaw, later called it the most satisfying win of his career.

It cannot be stressed enough just how badly the Bills trounced the Steelers that day, and just how much of an accomplishment that seemed at the time, even if the Pittsburgh dynasty would turn out to be in its final throes.

The Bills notched four sacks and hurried Bradshaw all day. Bradshaw was eventually knocked out of the game in the fourth quarter. Essential Steel Curtain component L.C. Greenwood left the game with cracked ribs. The vaunted Steelers receiving corps was completely shut down, with half of Bradshaw's 17 completions coming on short dumpoffs to Franco Harris or Rocky Bleier. Mario Clark spent much of the game making life difficult for Lynn Swann. Earlier that week, Swann had made some negative comments about the Bills defense, even though at the time it was statistically No. 1 in the NFL. Cribbs rushed for 110 yards, the first running back to go over 100 against the Steelers defense for the year.

Dozens of extra police and security guards had been assembled in and around Rich Stadium in anticipation of fights breaking out between warring packs of fans, but in the end, there were very few serious incidents. The Steelers fans, shocked as they were, had to hand it to the Buffalonians. Even Mean Joe Greene admitted that the Bills had whipped them.

Four days later, on Thanksgiving Day, a hearty snowfall blanketed the Buffalo area, making for some great TFL, but also for some slippery road conditions for those people trying to get to grandma's for the holiday. Western New Yorkers were used to long winters, so a Turkey Day storm, while not all that common, was taken in stride. Besides, there was so much for which to be thankful. After all, the Bills were 9–3 and in first place.

CHAPTER EIGHT

CURTAIN CALL

That a jangly little tune like "Talking Proud" would become the Bills anthem was unlikely enough, but equally curious was the fact that the song took hold more than halfway through a season in which the players *already had* a theme song. Bellowed out in the locker room after each win, this off-tempo number called "I Got a Feeling" was the creation of defensive lineman Ken "Baby" Johnson and had even fewer lyrics than the Chamber of Commerce's hit song. Johnson's went:

> *"I got a feeling*
> *That Buffalo's going to the Super Bowl*
> *It won't be the last time*
> *But Buffalo's going to the Super Bowl"*

In one memorable NFL Films clip, Isiah Robertson performs Johnson's song, a cappella, in the Bills locker room, crooning in almost a hesitant whisper, a playful smile on his face.

Johnson, a hopeless stutterer who grew up in Nashville, modeled his song after a disco hit of the time (possibly "Got A Feeling" by Frenchman Patrick Juvet).

The song had come bursting out of his big apple cheeks spontaneously (like many stutterers, Johnson's tongue didn't get tied when singing) after the Week 1 win over the Dolphins. It immediately caught on with Mario Clark and Charlie Romes, who sang right along, and by Week 2 "I Got A Feeling" was raucously belted out by more than half of the players in the locker room. Eventually, the entire team sang it after victories throughout the year.

Interestingly, Baby Johnson wasn't the only Bill to come up with a song that year. Even as Talking Proud swept the area, Lou Piccone, who had his own off-season lounge act singing George Benson covers at the Executive Inn out by the Buffalo Airport, had recorded the timeless classic "Ain't Nobody Gonna Buffalo My Bills." Sweet Lou's song got a fair amount of local airplay on KB Radio 1520 AM, even though that autumn it seemed as if there was a law requiring at least one station play "My Baby Takes the Morning Train" by Sheena Easton or "Sailing" by Christopher Cross at all times.

Other football teams had musical themes as well, new takes on the old traditional fight songs. A year earlier the Tampa Bay Buccaneers came out with a song, "Hey Hey Tampa Bay," during their own Cinderella season. Starting out 5–0, the Bucs, only a few years removed from the winless 1976 season and the mind-boggling 26-game losing streak that lasted well into 1977, remarkably had made it to the NFC Championship game played January 6, 1980. The Bucs lost, 9–0, in a teeming rainstorm to the Rams.

Kids in my neighborhood, while Bills fans, were sometimes prone to singing other team's songs, often during TFL play, but only if they were catchy enough. For example, the Downey brothers, Bobby and Jimmy, were big Earl Campbell fans, so they loved to sing the Houston Oilers song. *"We're the Houston Oilers! Houston Oilers!"* they'd sing in unison as we made our way to Wilson Farms for five-cent "little hugs" after Potter Road tackle football games. I can also recall Mike Gallivan, the eldest Gallivan brother and a TFL forefather, jokingly crooning the "San Diego Super Chargers" song from time to time.

These songs, battle cries really, were expressly tied to football, designed to stir the fans. In the late 1970s, the Oilers rolled out a new slogan, "Love Ya Blue." More of a catchphrase than a musical number, the phenomenon swept up the Houston area. At the culmination of the 1978 season, some 50,000 Oiler fans, many of them wearing t-shirts and holding signs that said "Love Ya Blue," gathered in the Astrodome to thank the team, which had been whipped in the AFC Championship by the Steelers, 34–5.

But Talking Proud ostensibly had nothing to do with football or the Bills. It only became associated with the team as a result of the Chamber's Pat Donlon convincing Bills PR man Budd Thalman to play the song at the Bills-Steelers game. After that, Talking Proud was a sensation.

The messages were run so often the Chamber was forced to fast-track plans to produce a second flight of commercials to avoid burn-out with the first series, already extended beyond what had been scheduled as a result of it catching fire. Many local companies started to incorporate the Talking Proud emblem into their business logos. Adam Meldrum and Anderson's downtown store sold thousands of $3 lapel pins, manufactured in Taiwan but obtained by the Chamber through merchandise wholesaler House of Sandburg on Main Street. A cottage industry sprang up in time for the holiday shopping season, at a time when Buffalo businesses were hurting. Domino Promotions on Grand Island was licensed to make neckties and scarves bearing the logo. Trench Manufacturing created pennants and buttons. Buffalo Shirt Factory produced sweatshirts, and New Era Cap Co. made hats. The Chamber signed deals with 20 area companies to make an array of products. There were canvas Talking Proud tote bags, coasters, tablecloths, stationery, pillow cases, ring binders, book covers, puzzles, paperweights, coffee mugs, plates, rubber stamps, oven mitts, coins, chocolates, you name it, even a Talking Proud board game a la Monopoly, only instead of Boardwalk and Park Place there was Delaware and Elmwood.

The campaign, aimed at lifting community spirits, had achieved its goal, and done so much more. It was now, forever, fittingly, connected with the Bills. But in an even further ironic twist surrounding the unexpected rise of the Talking Proud phenomenon, a local supermarket had at the time also tried, but failed, to come out with a promotional gimmick to rally fans. We're talking weenie, as in the bizarrely conceived "Whammy Weenie."

Loosely inspired by perhaps the "Terrible Towel," or possibly the baseball Pittsburgh Pirates' Green Weenie Whammy of the mid-1960s, these dark green plastic hotdogs were for fans to wave and rattle, to put the "whammy" on opponents, but they were quickly banned when it became evident that the tiny lead balls contained within the weenie (so as to make them rattle) were potentially poisonous and prone to shooting out the top when flung, rendering them dangerous, shard-spewing hazards. Bells, the local supermarket chain which had co-sponsored the promotion, did not antici-pate that deviously inclined fans would mutilate them. Bells CEO Chuck Barcelona, a noted community leader, caught his share of flak over the whole fiasco and the weenies were recalled and banned at the stadium. But the real mystery still remains: Why were the weenies *green*?

The Bills win over the Steelers cast a glow over all of Buffalo as the holidays approached. It was a glorious feeling to know the team was marching toward the playoffs. A lot of people were thinking Super Bowl, and why not?

Well, for starters, one week after the Steelers game the Bills were defeated for the second time that season by the Baltimore Colts, a game that saw five turnovers on special teams. The Bills also blew a 14-point lead. It was one of those 2 P.M. starts they used to have at Memorial Stadium in Baltimore. I always felt there was something off kilter about those delayed starts.

So when Chuck Knox's old team, the Los Angeles Rams, came into Rich Stadium on Sunday, December 7th, the game took on an even greater importance. The Patri-ots were clawing right up our ass, and so the Bills could not afford a loss, especially not at home. This one was al-ready penciled in on the calendar as a big game. Not only had Knox and practically his entire staff come from the Rams, the Bills had three ex-Rams on their team. Knox had long wanted this game. Now he needed it.

I remembered delivering papers that Sunday morning, and selling a few extras on the corner of Ridge Road and Abbott as fans made their way out to the stadium. I'd sold just enough to generate proceeds for a McDonalds feast. The one on Ridge near South Shore Boulevard, which comprised the bulk of my paper route, had the authentic Golden Arches built into the retro storefront, right out of the 1950s. But nothing beat the McDonalds on Orchard Park Road, not far from Rich Stadium. It was a regular McDonalds, only it was completely decked out with Buffalo Bills regalia and NFL imagery, plastering the walls and tabletops. On Sundays, my dad used to take me and my brothers, Tommy and Shawn, to St. Martin's Church for 10:30 A.M. Mass, and he told us we could earn McDonalds privileges if we sang the hymns loudly enough. We called it the "Bills McDonalds." On home Sundays, we could feel the Rich Stadium excitement just being in there.

As I choked back my post-Sunday-paper-route Egg McMuffins, I had but one thing on my mind—getting to the Bills game. By around 11 A.M. I'd made my way over to the Gallivan's house. I tried to convince Timmy Gallivan to go with me out to the stadium, but it was cold and rainy and he just wasn't up for it. But I had a plan.

Starting that summer, some of my other buddies and I had begun to assemble a formidable beer can collection. It wasn't long before we'd be sneaking around Caz Park with full cans of beer, but in seventh grade we hunted for empty ones. I had pooled my can collection with those of three friends, Tommy McDonnell, Brian George and Pat Keane, creating a supercollection which toured each of our basements by way of a joint custody arrangement.

Late to the can fad, but no less enthusiastic, was Timmy Gallivan. He was starting up a collection of his own. I remember wanting so badly to go to the Bills/Rams game as the clock neared 1 P.M., but not having the nerve to head out there alone. I finally sold Timmy on the concept of going out to the stadium purely to pick up beer cans. He agreed, and soon we were up on Abbott Road across from the Towne Movie Theatre (1980 was the heyday of the Towne's 99-cent Monday night slasher flicks, including that summer's "Friday the 13th" and "Prom Night") with our thumbs out. Eventually, someone who knew my brother Danny gave us a lift and by game time we were circling the stadium. Timmy was still building the core of his collection, cans I couldn't be bothered with—Schmidts, Blatz, Carlsberg, Labbatt's 50, Old Vienna, Genny, Genny "Cold Aged," Genny Light, Genny Cream Ale—so he was having a bonanza, but I still needed to convince him to go to the game. The atmosphere outside the stadium was both exhilarating and intimidating, but somehow there seemed to be safety in numbers. By the time we made our way to the gates, the game had already started. One small obstacle left to overcome—Timmy didn't want to leave his cans. I finally persuaded him to dump them. It was raining on and off, and getting foggy. Through the turnstiles trickled the last of the fans making their way in midway through the first quarter. Timmy and I started looking for his father, who was taking tickets that day.

Mr. Gallivan was a soft-spoken mailman who was always building a new addition or gardening or fixing something. He had a great record collection (The Beach Boys "Live in London," the Beatles' "Rubber Soul," all the Bill Cosby comedy records) and turned us kids on to "SCTV" on Canadian television, as well as lots of great old monster movies on Channel 9, WOR out of New York, such as the original "King Kong" and "Mighty Joe Young." Every day after completing his mail route, Mr. Gallivan would come home, sit at the kitchen table and have one beer out of a frosted pint glass while catching up with Mrs. Gallivan on the day's events.

As we circled the stadium perimeter, Timmy and I couldn't find him. He was a sure-fire way into the stadium, but he must have left early. Eventually, we found Mr. McLeary, another one of the neighborhood dads who was also a ticket-taker (all part of the ticket-taker and usher's union run by South Buffalo's Bill Greeley). With a thick red walrus mustache, Mr. McLeary was an unemployed steel worker, quiet but intimidating. You knew by his eyes he was someone you never wanted to piss off. I remember once Mr. McLeary teaching his son Paulie a valuable lesson. Paulie, a few years younger than me, got his bike stolen (an unwritten rule, every kid in Buffalo is obligated to have at least one bike ripped off) by this little punk Jackie Smith. Jackie lived down the block on Maryon Drive near the spooky Egan apartments, red-brick asylums for low-income elderly, with a smattering of freaks, villains and other assorted characters. When Paulie McLeary, a shy boy, came home crying about his bike being stolen, Mr. McLeary marched him down to Jackie's house and told him not to come out without the bike. Jackie was a pipsqueak, even younger than Paulie, but he was a fireplug, with a mean streak, and he slapped the shit out of Paulie, sending him running for his father. Mr. McLeary, standing in front of Jackie's house on the sidewalk, ordered his bloody-nosed son to do as he'd been told, to go back and get the bike. No matter how many times Jackie flailed away, and no matter how hard Paulie begged to end the episode, Mr. McLeary stood quietly on the sidewalk. "You aren't leaving without that bike," he told his son. Finally, Paulie summoned the will and he somehow pulled it off—he pummeled Jackie into submission and took back his property.

Anyway, Mr. McLeary gladly let Timmy and I sneak in, and by the time we made it inside the stadium the Bills-Rams game was well underway.

The Bills defense was playing the game of their life. In the chilly mist of that early December afternoon, the Rams became hunted prey, stalked violently by a blood-lusting Buffalo squad determined to win this game for Chuck Knox. Rams quarterback Vince Ferragamo— who'd been on the cover of that week's *Sports Illustrated* with the headline "Ram Power"—was mauled in the second quarter by Ben Williams. Later, Ferragamo left the game with broken ribs.

Backup Pat Haden came in the game but struggled, getting dumped violently by Bills defensive lineman Mike Kadish. In the third quarter Haden tossed a costly interception. Bills free safety Steve Freeman stepped in front of the pass and went 47 yards down the left sideline for the first score of the game.

While the Bills offense couldn't get it going, the defense gladly took the entire team upon its shoulders.

"We will stop them every time, all day, for however long it takes!" captain Shane Nelson was screaming on the sidelines. After yet another three and out, Haslett ran on the field and told a frustrated Ferguson not to worry. "Hey, I'll beat on these guys all day—this is fun!"

The Bills defense would have to make good on that vow.

This game should have been out of reach long ago. In the first half, Mike-Mayer missed two field goals. Part of the problem was that center Will Grant was playing with a broken hand, and in the damp weather the ball was slippery. Then again, Mike-Mayer was able to get his kicks off, they just hadn't been accurate. In the second half, Knox doubled down, deep in Rams territory, twice opting to go for it on fourth and short yardage rather than kick a field goal. Both times the Bills came away with no points. Partially, it was Mike-Mayer's first half problems, but Knox wanted to strike a death blow and trusted his line. On one of those gambles, Cribbs was stopped on fourth down at the Rams 8. On another, Leaks fumbled the ball into the Rams end zone where it was recovered by defensive back Nolan Cromwell.

As the clock ticked down, instead of the game being out of reach, the Rams had time for one last drive. They'd had no business being on the field with the Bills all day. They had been utterly dominated. They'd been held to 34 yards passing. The Rams should have been ready to limp back to the West Coast for some sun and relaxation, leaving the bone-chilling misery of the "Armpit of the East" behind them. But to the Rams' credit, they proceeded to march the length of the field, a 14-play drive aided by long runs by Mike Guman, a rookie back out of Penn State. The drive culminated in a three-yard Guman touchdown run.

The game was tied, 7–7.

By this time, late in the fourth quarter, overtime drawing near, I was on my own. Timmy had left at half-time to go look for his cans, but I stayed behind. I was freezing, soaked and a little bit nervous, but this game was just too important. I set out to make my way through the stands to the section below the press box, under cover of the upper deck, offering me protection from the persistent drizzle. The temperature was around 40 degrees and falling.

I was starting to wish that Timmy hadn't left, and found myself wandering the hallways until I finally came across my brother Danny, who had worked that day as an usher. It was good to see a familiar face. Most of the ushers had already left, but Danny, still clad in his red usher's jacket, had stayed on through regulation serving as a cheerleader for his section. He was animated, excited, showing no sign of worry whatsoever heading into the extra period. Overtime in the regular season had been instituted by the league in 1974, so this was only the second overtime game in Bills history.

When the Rams won the coin toss, Danny brought us all calm, yelling, with a wild grin, over and over, "We're gonna stop them!" He genuinely seemed as happy to have me there as I was to have found him. As much as Danny was confident, I was nervous. On this morose day when the Bills had squandered an easy win, it seemed to me their punishment would be to lose. Danny had it the other way around, I could tell, and I started to believe. He seemed to have the whole section believing that the Bills were destined to win this game.

On the field, Frank Lewis was in agonizing pain. Two weeks earlier he'd sprained his back against the Steelers. He'd been replaced by Ron Jessie. Lewis was not expected to play against the Rams. He hadn't practiced all week. But the morning of the game Lewis begged Knox for his starting position. Despite his aching back, he'd already hauled in a pair of big receptions from Ferguson, but Lewis' biggest catch was still yet to come.

The Rams, as we hoped, were forced to punt. On second and ten, from just inside Ram territory, Ferguson hit Lewis on the sideline. Lewis and one of the Rams cornerbacks went up for a jump ball, but it was Lewis who came down with it, splashing down the sidelines as the crowd rose to their feet. It was a 30-yard play, and suddenly, five minutes into the overtime session, the Bills were in business.

Twice burned by opting not to kick a field goal, Knox didn't hesitate. He sent in his kicker right away. Center Will Grant steadied his throbbing hand. Earlier that morning he had sawed off his cast. His holder, David Humm, the third-string quarterback, tried to keep him calm. "We're going to hit this," Humm said as they set up.

The Rams called timeout. They were trying to ice Mike-Mayer. On WBEN radio, Van Miller used the pause to build a spine-tingling sense of tension as darkness fell.

"And now it's up to Nick Mike-Mayer. The crowd murmurs with anticipation. Mike-Mayer waiting. Waiting. Waiting for the snap. Waiting for the snap is David Humm. *Waiting.*"

In the stands, 77,000 or so fans held their breath. Mike-Mayer, aiming from 30 yards away, stood ready.

Grant's snap was flawless. Humm handled it clean. The kick sailed through the fog and the rain, and . . . straight through the uprights!

The Talking Proud song cued and at that very moment Rich Stadium lit up like no one had ever seen before. Rising 30 feet in the night air, more than 100 feet long, stood the old Bills CONRAC scoreboard. In its heyday, this scoreboard was among the most technically advanced in the world. With a computerized matrix of nearly 10,000 40-watt light bulbs, it produced what today would be considered crude instant replays. Like a giant Lite Brite, the scoreboard danced with an electrified "Talking Proud" emblem.

As the Bills fans celebrated, the song played on an endless loop. When it reached the crescendo, all the bulbs lit up like gold, filling the stadium with a warm, shimmering light. Danny and I jumped and laughed as the image flickered. Down in the end zone, the rowdies were screaming for Mike-Mayer, and soon the whole stadium was chanting his name.

The scoreboard crew asked Bills assistant PR man Mike Shaw if they should cut the tape. He told them, "What the heck, *keep playing it.*"

Sure enough Mike-Mayer came running back through the tunnel, throwing his arms high above his head. But the celebration was just getting underway.

Shaw, who'd stayed behind in the press box, called down to the locker room where Budd Thalman had gone to supervise the post-game interviews.

"What should we do?" Shaw asked.

"What are you talking about?" Thalman responded.

"No one is leaving."

Thalman had an idea. The Bills would make a curtain
call. Thalman quickly passed word to assistant trainer
Bud Tice, who in turn agreed to rustle up some of the
players. The first player Tice saw was a jubilant Reggie
McKenzie, more than happy to oblige. McKenzie
rounded up some other cohorts, about 20 or so, who
came barreling out of the tunnel clad in gray t-shirts and
sweatshirts, some without pads, some still in uniform.
The cheerleaders, known as The Jills, had been doing a
kickline by the end zone wall as the fans clapped and
sang along with the Talking Proud song that had been
blaring over the public address system continuously.
Fred Smerlas was carrying his buddy Jim Haslett
around the field piggyback. After circling the end zones
slapping high fives, the Bills contingent—among them
Smerlas, Haslett, Ben Williams, Dee Hardison, Conrad
Dobler, Phil Villapiano, Chris Keating and Baby Johnson—joined The Jills in their chorus line, performing a
Can-Can as effortlessly as the Radio City Hall Rockettes.
The Bills were 10–4. Ten wins—that was the most wins
in any season since 1965.

The misty day got even mistier. In a luxury suite, not
far from Ralph Wilson's, Chamber chairman Andy
Craig looked out at the scoreboard flashing the Talking
Proud logo in fluorescent gold, and thought back to all
the effort that had gone into producing the campaign.
All he'd wanted was for Buffalonians to feel good about
their hometown. As the song played, and the fans sang
along, tears of joy filled Craig's eyes.

In the Bills locker room Isiah Robertson sat shaking
his head, emotionally drained. Robertson thought that
he'd hit bottom when the Rams banished him to Buffalo,

and despite his off-the-field escapades and personal demons he was coming to realize what a special town he'd become a part of. With the weight of the world lifted from his shoulders, as reporters looked on, he openly wept.

Not far away, a special visitor had found her way into the basement of Rich Stadium. It was Knox's wife, Shirley, the quiet Huntingdon, Pa. high school cheerleader who'd caught Chuck's eye at a dancehall back in his Juniata College days. Like a scene out of "Rocky," Shirley Knox forced her way through security, and into the area outside the locker room. When she saw her husband, she rushed into his arms and gave him a kiss. She'd been there through it all. She'd seen her husband run out of Los Angeles. "Oh Chuck, I'm just so proud of everyone!" she told him as they embraced, teardrops streaming down her cheeks.

Even Knox got a bit teary-eyed a short while later when his players gathered around him and presented *him* with the game ball.

"This one was for you," Dobler said, handing it to Knox, the entire team cheering and whistling.

The Bills had battled, scratched, clawed, fought, had done whatever it took to win that game and they'd done it for him. Knox had never seen such intensity. He'd never been more proud of his men.

That night the glory of Buffalo sports only continued. As it turned out, my brother was also scheduled to usher the evening's 7 P.M. Sabres game against the St. Louis Blues at Memorial Auditorium. We drove home from the stadium together in his '75 Chevy Nova hatchback, and after a quick change of clothes and some Abbott pizza, headed off to The Aud. My brother Shawn joined us, and Danny set up folding chairs for us right behind the goalie, my best vantage point at a major sporting event ever. The Sabres won. I'd witnessed first-hand a precious two-win day in Buffalo.

The sheer thrill of victory, the coming Christmas season, it was more happiness than I even needed. I remember laying in bed that night, thinking how my day had started seemingly forever ago, delivering Sunday papers at 6 A.M. It seemed like it couldn't have been just one day, but it was. And I've never forgotten it.

CHAPTER NINE

OUT OF THE MUD, CHAMPIONS

The following night after the Bills dramatic overtime win against the Rams at Rich Stadium, the second-place Patriots were playing the Dolphins on *Monday Night Football*. Danny was downstairs in the basement convincing me of the significance of this game. I'd assumed the Bills were sitting pretty; he explained to me that yes, they would be if the Patriots lost, because then they would be two games behind the Bills in the AFC East with two games to play. If the Patriots won, however, they were still very much alive. In fact, the Bills were set to play the Patriots in New England on Sunday.

Quarterbacked by Steve Grogan, these red-and-white Pats were an upper-echelon franchise, respected if not feared. They had a pretty wide open offense featuring speedy wide receiver Stanley Morgan and tight end Russ Francis. Between 1976 and 1980 the Pats would win 50 games, among the most in the NFL during that period. But in their two playoff appearances, the Pats lost both games.

So our alliance on this night, uncharacteristically, was with the Dolphins. But alas, whereas I had been free to roam the city the day before, the clamps had now come down—hard. No negotiating; I was not allowed to stay up to watch the game, ordered to bed by my mother over vociferous objection. I lay awake upstairs, brooding, restless, convinced that unless the Dolphins beat the Patriots, all would not be right with the world.

Finally, after at least two hours had passed, when I was sure my mother was fast asleep, I tip-toed downstairs, where Danny was watching the game, by now into the fourth quarter.

As it turned out, all was not right with the world. Danny saw me crouching on the stairs in my pajamas and before I could ask for the score he blurted out the news which Howard Cosell had just relayed to a stunned country.

"Somebody shot John Lennon!"

Cosell got the scoop first because a WABC-TV news producer named Alan Weiss had crashed his motorcycle into a taxi in Central Park earlier that night, and had wound up in the emergency room of Roosevelt Hospital when Lennon was brought in. Weiss managed to stagger over to a telephone, and minutes later, Cosell interrupted the game with the tragic news that the 40-year-old ex-Beatle was dead. The normally brash commentator gave a short, solemn tribute to Lennon, and then respectfully resumed to play by play as the Patriots got a first down.

It was sad. The Beatles were a favorite in my house, rather, my garage, which in the summertime became something of a beachfront cabana, replete with carpet, portable TV, old New York Yankees photos—Ruth, Mantle, DiMaggio—JFK and RFK campaign posters, a clumsy 8-track stereo and a beautiful, vintage barber chair. The Beatles 8-tracks (particularly the early stuff, "Love Me Do," "She Loves You," "I Want to Hold Your Hand," "Please Please Me," "8 Days a Week") seemed to play endlessly in the summer. I knew the words to all of those Beatles songs before I could even talk. I cherished my Red and Blue albums, and Lennon being killed was tragically depressing news. The Dolphins did end up beating the Patriots in overtime that night, 16–13 on an Uwe von Schaman field goal, but I can't say that I remember much else about the game.

I do recall the next day at school that my fellow classmates did not seem able to relate to my grief. I commiserated with one of the few who could, Mike Dwyer, a tall, husky eighth grader who played drums in a rock band, The Scum, and who drank beers on Lockey's Hill with the high school kids. That year we were in a reading class together. We'd created a fictitious cartoon rock group called "Atomic Head." I would literally piss my navy blue school uniform pants as Dwyer passed me his wickedly funny drawings of fake album covers and his sketches of various band members. We both loved The Who, but Dwyer steadily had been introducing me to new groups, such as The Specials, The Clash and The Jam.

"You like the Beatles, right?" I'd asked him, and I recall him saying, "Of course."

Lennon's murder had slightly dampened my high spirits. What happened to the Bills on Sunday, December 14th at Schaefer Stadium against the New England Patriots would completely crush them.

On a cold day with a chance to clinch the division the Bills got off on the wrong foot, figuratively and then literally. On the opening kickoff, Curtis Brown bobbled the ball. It rolled out of bounds at the Bills 2-yard line. The Bills couldn't get anything going, and punted. The Patriots took over at the Bills 41, needing only a few plays to take a 7–0 lead.

On the next series, the game just nine minutes old, Ferguson called an audible, a handoff to Cribbs, only Cribbs misheard the signal. When Ferguson went to hand the ball off to Cribbs, he wasn't there. So, Fergy ate it—except blitzing linebacker Mike Hawkins wasn't about to let the Bills quarterback off so easily. He stormed into the backfield and came down on Ferguson cleanly, like an iron on the collar of a shirt. Ferguson dropped, all his weight imploding on his left ankle, which buckled.

No, not Joe, McKenzie thought looking back at his quarterback writhing in pain on the turf.

All of Buffalo shared the same thought. Fergy left the game. He did not return.

Ferguson's replacement was Dan Manucci. Apart from holding on field goals in his rookie year of 1979, Manucci, by the late part of the season of 1980, had taken just one snap. It had come earlier in the year, against the Colts. Knox had Fergy pretend to have a chin-strap malfunction so he could sneak the faster Manucci into the game. Knox creatively tried to catch the Colts playing back in a zone defense on second and long. Manucci was to roll out, get outside and zip up-field for the five or so yards that on paper were supposed to be his for the taking. But the Colts switched to man coverage and Manucci went nowhere. That had been the sum of his NFL career.

The Bills had been the least sacked team in the league; a mere 12 of them allowed coming into that game against the Patriots. Manucci, who had speed, and who loved to scramble, would be sacked five times. One sack he took on fourth down, strictly taboo even in Pop Warner. Knox benched him and put in David Humm. He would fare no better. Humm was sacked three times. Those 8 sacks practically doubled the Bills total for the season in one game.

New England soundly spanked the Bills, 24–2, their lone points coming when Patriots punter Mike Hubach, recipient of a high snap, was tackled in the end zone by Bill Simpson and Rufus Bess.

That night at the Westinghouse Electric Company parking lot adjacent to the Greater Buffalo Airport, a podium had been set up with a microphone, and thousands of fans were preparing to greet the Bills, assuming they were coming home with the AFC East championship.

In 14-degree weather some 500 fans actually showed up anyway, bearing signs, including one that said "It's OK—We're Still Talking Proud!" In fact, as the fans stood around freezing, waiting for the Bills' plane to land (their flight had been delayed by an hour and didn't land until 8:30 P.M.), they sang the Talking Proud song. When the players did finally arrive, they were touched by what they saw. Reggie McKenzie shouted: "Don't worry, we are going out to San Francisco to kick their ass!"

The entire season now came down to this one last regular season game against the 6–9 San Francisco 49ers at Candlestick Park. The 49ers were coming off two straight 2–14 seasons and at one point had lost seven straight in 1980. But they were suddenly showing life under a second-year quarterback from Notre Dame named Joe Montana. If the Bills were defeated, and the Patriots beat the Saints, the Bills would lose the tiebreaker because they had a worse divisional record. After this incredibe season there was the distinct possibility that the Bills could *miss* the postseason, or that they could finish 11–5 and win the division—all or nothing.

Winter arrived in earnest that week and the indoor bubble facility had not yet been built, so Knox arranged to fly the team out to Stanford University's facilities in Palo Alto to practice. Before the flight, the offensive line as a unit summoned assistant coach Ray Prochaska and informed him that they would not block for Dan Manucci. "We have no confidence in him," Dobler told his offensive line coach.

Ferguson's ankle was in bad shape, so he spent the week rehabbing (ice/massage/heat/ice). Manucci took nearly every snap in practice, and by Saturday afternoon, with Ferguson still limping around as he took his first snaps of the week, it looked doubtful he would play.

Dobler had demanded that Knox start third-string quarterback David Humm, except that Knox and quarterback coach Kay Stephenson had no confidence in Humm. Ferguson, it was decided, would have to play if he could. That was the team's best chance. Ferguson told Stephenson Sunday morning, "Aw heck, just tape it up."

Back at the Hyatt in downtown San Francisco, as Manucci was getting ready to leave his room for the bus to Candlestick Park, he received a strange telephone call. The voice on the other end claimed to be a reporter for a paper in Kansas. "Are you starting today?" the voice queried. Manucci had been told by Stephenson to be ready, but had never officially been informed one way or the other. "I guess it's going to be a game time decision," Manucci replied. With that, the caller quickly hung up. Later, on the bus, Manucci's roommate David Humm, who'd grown up in Las Vegas, asked about the call. "You idiot! That was no reporter—that was a bookie!"

The decision to start Ferguson was made in pre-game warm-ups. He would gut it out.

One Bills player who figured for sure he wouldn't be seeing any action on the field was Villapiano. He'd played just a handful of downs. All year long, Knox kept telling the veteran to be prepared to go in at any time, at any side. That week the only thing Villapiano prepared for was to visit all of his favorite haunts in the Bay Area, staying out late and partying for five straight nights leading up to the game. Dobler proved to be an eager companion.

Two nights before the big game, Villapiano, Dobler and Bob Moore, a former teammate of Villapiano with the Raiders, who at the time was studying at Stanford Law School, went out drinking right after dinner. They wanted to be back in time for bed check, 11 P.M., for no other reason than that they did not want to let Knox down. On the way back to the hotel around 10 P.M. Dobler got pulled over by the cops. At some point they asked him to count backwards from 100. He launched into a rendition of "99 bottles of beer on the wall." Villapiano, shitfaced from too many shots of whiskey and tequila in too short a time frame, ended up telling the cops to fuck off. "Take me to jail officers, do what you must but please . . . ," said Dobler, pointing to Villapiano, ". . . whatever you do, do not let that man drive me home." Surprisingly, the cops let them go, and they made it back in time for bedcheck.

But the next morning, Knox was none too pleased to see their bloodshot eyes at practice, and told them, "Remember, we've got a game tomorrow. You might want to temper your behavior a bit."

When Sunday finally arrived it did so with heavy rains that began just before kickoff and continued throughout the game, turning Candlestick Park into a four-inch-thick mud bath. It would be that much harder for Ferguson, already crippled, to move around in such a quagmire, that much more labor intensive for Dobler to lift his wobbly, battered legs.

Gathered in my Tudor Boulevard basement were most of the TFL gang, me, my brother Shawn, the Gallivans and the Robertsons. Seeing Fergy take the field was a confidence boost and a surprise development, as we'd been told all week that he likely wouldn't play. Early in the game we had even more of a reason to be happy: On the first play, Joe Cribbs took a handoff in a steady rain, and on blocks by Curtis Brown and Ken Jones, rambled 48 yards down the left sideline. That run, longest of the season, set up a perfectly thrown 10-yard touchdown pass from Ferguson to Butler in the left corner of the end zone as he was pushed out of bounds. The Bills, after a missed conversion, led 6–0.

Unfortunately, the Bills had a bad break on the first defensive series; literally—linebacker Shane Nelson dislocated his left wrist, pinned under San Francisco lineman Randy Cross.

"Villapiano you're in," defensive coordinator Tom Catlin told him on the sidelines.

One problem: Nelson was the defensive captain and called the formations. Villapiano didn't know any of Catlin's signals. Catlin told him not to worry. "You call the defense."

When he got in the huddle, Villapiano's role as player/coach took on new meaning. He'd talked some serious smack all year, and while the players ate it up and loved having him around, he knew by the looks in their eyes that he had better be able to back it up. Villapiano rose to the challenge, and began making more tackles than anyone else on the field.

The 49ers, led by the rookie Montana, and their own star rookie running back, Earl Cooper, responded with a 9-play, 77-yard drive that culminated in a questionable touchdown. Cooper appeared to lose control of the ball as he stumbled into the end zone from the four. The replay showed he clearly fumbled before going over the goal line, but somewhat soothing the burn of the bogus touchdown was the fact that 49ers kicker Ray Wersching missed the point-after-touchdown, making the score 6–6.

Operating gingerly out of the shotgun, Ferguson, who hadn't practiced all week, zipped the Bills down the field, and a Curtis Brown run from the four-yard-line followed by a successful extra-point kick gave the Bills a 13–6 lead at the half.

But the 49ers tied the game on the strength of their rookies. Cooper broke one, and this Joe Montana kid was showing poise, hitting Eason Ramson for the game-tying touchdown. Later in the third quarter, Buffalo had a call go its way when Frank Lewis ran a deep pattern and drew an interference penalty, probably a make-up for the blown call on the 49ers questionable touchdown. That led to a Mike-Mayer field goal. Later, Baby Johnson tackled 49ers punter Jim Miller in the end zone for a safety, making the score 18–13.

But Montana and the 49ers weren't rolling over. They drove the ball late in the fourth quarter, deep into Bills territory. They were going to score, I was sure of it.

With each Montana pass (*who was this guy?*) my stomach tightened. I shuddered as the 49ers inched closer. Now they were on the Bills 8-yard line and I began to get hysterical. This fabulous, magical season was going up in flames. "They're going to score!" I cried out to my friends gathered in my basement. "We're going to lose!" I was profoundly distraught. Right then, the 49ers running back Earl Cooper fumbled, after a jarring hit by Lucius Sanford. Bills cornerback Mario Clark had recovered!

Tears of agony transformed into those of happiness, and everyone in the basement seemed relieved, and even a little happy for me. "You can stop crying now," Shawn said. "I told you not to worry," John Gallivan said. To say now looking back that the other kids watching the game along with me had more confidence in the outcome, less fear, would be an understatement. The Bills were life and death to me. Emotionally, I was all in. The subsequent scene in my basement, nervous laughter, talk of playoffs, was relaxed as the Bills took over with the clock waning.

But when the 49ers ended up somehow getting the

ball at midfield, our jovial banter ceased and we were all suddenly gripped by fear. The game, it seemed, was not over. Nine seconds remained. Possibly the longest nine seconds of my life.

The first Montana Hail Mary hung up in the air for an agonizing eternity and came down in slow motion. It was painful to watch. This should not have even been happening—*the game was over*.

At the end of Montana's rainbow, in the left corner of the end zone, was wide receiver Charlie Young. The ball was right in his hands. I swear I saw him—he had it in his hands. Mario Clark, who thought he'd saved the game with his fumble recovery, saw Young catch it too, and he almost had a heart attack. The whole season was coming down to this unbelievable ending. But someone was looking out for the Bills—Charlie Romes. He drilled Young just at that moment he had the ball in his clutches, and it plopped down into the soup.

Time for one more Hail Mary.

No tears on my end, just a petrified stupor. We were all standing now and yelling, red-faced, emotional, looking at each other half-shocked, *could this really be happening*?

Montana dropped back. The Bills pass rush was valiant, the soggy players' feet sinking into the turf as they drove their legs. Montana let the ball sail. On the one hand, I remember thinking as it flew through the air, *well they'd just had their chance.* Desperation jump balls almost never work out. But at the same time, there was this funny feeling that doom lurked. All we could do was watch. The ball was batted around. Hearts stopped. And then finally the ball fell harmlessly to the ground.

On the field, Villapiano and Smerlas wallowed around in the mud, laughing, like little kids, and on Tudor we kids laughed and hugged and wallowed in the majesty of a moment no one ever could have predicted at the beginning of the season.

Christmas had come a little early. The Buffalo Bills were AFC East Champions.

CHAPTER TEN

HEARTBREAK AT JACK MURPHY STADIUM

Three days before Christmas some 8,000 shivering fans were waiting at the airport to greet the AFC East Champion Buffalo Bills. It was now Monday morning, December 22, at 3:30 A.M., in 13-degree temperatures, but the fans were there.

It had been 14 long years since the Bills last won a division title. LBJ was President, The Beatles were just entering their psychedelic stage and the American Football League comprised just two divisions, the East—Buffalo, Boston, New York, Houston and Miami—and the West—Kansas City, Oakland, San Diego and Denver.

On Sunday, December 18, 1966, the Bills beat those Denver Broncos at War Memorial, 38–21, to clinch a third straight Eastern division crown. A day earlier, the still-contending Boston Patriots had lost to the Jets, 38–28, to finish 8–4–2. So the Bills, at 8–4–1, had known going into that game that a victory against the Broncos would give them the division, as well as a shot at the AFL Championship, and even more enticingly, a chance to appear in the first interleague championship game against the best team from the NFL.

Unlike in area native Vincent Gallo's film, "Buffalo 66," which as part of its backstory features a Scott Norwood-inspired fateful field goal gaffe to wreck the campaign, the real '66 Bills missed their date with destiny not by a few points in the waning seconds, but in a full-fledged drubbing at the hands of the Kansas City Chiefs, 31–7, at The Rockpile, ending the team's two-year reign over the AFL. The Chiefs went on to lose to the Green Bay Packers in Super Bowl I. The AFL and NFL merged in 1970 with the Bills being assigned to the AFC East.

While Buffalo fans would eventually become blasé about the Bills winning the AFC East—by the early 1990s it was a given—the hearty troopers who'd assembled at the airport in late December 1980 were there to savor every last drop of division title glory, waving signs that bore phrases such as "Champs" and "Super Bowl Bound." Today, the Erie County Parks Department may not have the budgetary means to fully staff Chestnut Ridge Park, but that night somebody from the department went the extra mile to set up a makeshift bandstand and a sound system which blared "Talking Proud" as fans danced around and drank beer, shouting out the lyrics into the frozen night.

"We appreciate what you've done for us," Coach Knox told the jubilant fans. "We love you!"

"I told you we were going to kick their asses!" hollered Reggie McKenzie.

The flight home from San Francisco had taken place with the Bills still not knowing who their foe would be in the upcoming divisional playoff in two weeks, but they knew a trip back out to California was a certainty. The playoff picture would be made clearer following the outcome of the final game of the regular season, that night, on *Monday Night Football*. The Chargers were playing the Steelers; if the Steelers won, the Raiders would win the AFC West, and the Chargers would be eliminated from the playoffs. The Patriots would sneak in as a wildcard, along with the Houston Oilers, already secure of a wildcard spot, and the Bills would be heading to Oakland. But if the Chargers won, they would win the AFC West (on the rare fifth tiebreaker "most net points within the division") and the Raiders would be awarded the second wildcard slot (installed in 1978), thus eliminating the Patriots.

So it was only fitting then that the Chargers beat the Steelers that Monday night, setting up the divisional playoff against the Bills. After all, it was in San Diego in 1965 that the Bills had tasted their last swig of AFL glory.

On the day after Christmas, in old Balboa Stadium, Buffalo quarterback Jack Kemp, No. 15, led the Bills to one of the most satisfying victories in the history of Western New York sports, a 23-0 spanking of the Chargers to win the AFL Championship. Kemp was named the MVP, but it was the Bills defense that sparkled in a game even more lopsided than the score might indicate.

That year the Chargers, favored by a touchdown to beat Buffalo at home, had led the AFL in passing yards on the wings of their graceful wide receiver Lance "Bambi" Alworth. The Bills, meanwhile, had lost their star receivers, Glenn Bass and Elbert Dubenion, earlier in the year to injuries, and had finished last in the league in passing.

Earlier that season, on Thanksgiving Day at Balboa Stadium, the Bills and Chargers played to a thrilling 20–20 tie. In the game's key play Alworth caught a bomb from quarterback John Hadl in the third quarter and was flying at light speed toward the end zone when somehow, defying space and time, the Bills defensive back Booker Edgerson caught up to Alworth and knocked the ball out of his hands a la Don Beebe, the Bills recovering in the end zone. Later, with just over a minute to play, Kemp, taking charge at the Bills 25, drove the team down the field for Pete Gogolak's 22-yard, game-tying kick with six seconds left.

The championship rematch was not as close. Lou Saban cooked up a holiday surprise, switching to a then little-used double tight end formation on offense and a daring, convention-snubbing 3–4 formation on defense, essentially unheard of back then. The Bills bumped Alworth all day, sometimes using five linebackers or an extra back, so much so that he barely finished half his routes.

Leading 7–0 with a little over two minutes in the half, the Bills return man Butch Byrd fielded a punt at the 26 and went racing up the sideline. His unlikely escort was lumbering punter Paul Maguire, best known today for providing ESPN Sunday night game commentary. At around the 15-yard line Maguire wiped out two last grasping Chargers with one thunderous block and Byrd was as free as one. The Bills never looked back.

Perhaps the singularly greatest momentum-shifting play in the history of the Bills—if not the NFL—also came against the Chargers, a year earlier in the 1964 AFL Championship, and also played the day after Christmas, this one at War Memorial Stadium.

The Chargers were the defending AFL Champions. They'd slaughtered the Patriots, 51–10, in the 1963 title game. The Bills had just won their first AFL East division with a victory over the Patriots in a blizzard at Fenway Park.

While both the Bills and the Chargers were preparing for arctic weather in Buffalo, somehow the conditions turned downright balmy and the game was played with temperatures reaching the 40s. The Chargers struck first with an 80-yard drive culminating in a touchdown pass and, following an ensuing Bills punt, were driving for another when it happened. Charger quarterback Tobin Rote looked to throw the ball deep but didn't see anyone open. Alworth had missed this game because of a leg injury, so running back Keith Lincoln, who'd scored four touchdowns in the 1963 championship rout over the Pats, was the go-to Charger. He'd scampered 38-yards on the first play from scrimmage, setting up the first Chargers score, and here he was darting unchaperoned into the left flat where Rote was looking to dump the ball off. Mike Stratton, the Bills 240-pound weakside linebacker, noticed Rote abandoning his search for a downfield receiver, and took his cue. Stratton sprinted for the wide open Lincoln, who was about to catch the ball.

One second earlier and Stratton would have been flagged for interference and one second later Stratton would have missed Lincoln altogether. But Stratton was punctual. He came with fury, slamming right-shoulder first into Lincoln's midsection with frightening force just as the ball arrived. Stratton rolled over and stood up unfazed. But the marvelous collision left a groaning Lincoln splattered on the turf, his ribs broken, lost for the game.

A visible shockwave went up and down the Bills

bench and the stadium belched ecstasy knowing with certainty the tide had turned. And it had. The Bills went on to score 20 unanswered points for their first AFL Championship.

So now the stage was set for another Bills/Chargers postseason showdown. Christmas was in the air. And a more glorious Christmas season I cannot recall. That Tuesday, with a snowstorm threatening, we had a half day of school followed by a holiday Mass across the street at St. Martin's Church. After Mass, all of the altar boys were called up one by one by our stern Pastor, Father Leon Neu, to receive little envelopes stuffed with $2 bills, $8 in total. When Mass was over, the students were free to go. It is difficult to begin to describe what an utterly joyous feeling it was, those first few moments of that particular Christmas vacation—rousing hymns still ringing in my ears (*Shepherds and Kings! Following hopes and stars that take them deeeeeeeeeep into the night!*) the crisp bills in my pocket, the skies grey, snow starting to fall, and best of all, the Bills were in the playoffs.

The whole town was feeling it. The next day, Christmas Eve, I recall watching Clip Smith, whose Channel 7 Eyewitness News at Noon sportscasts featured his "Clipley's Believe it Don't" gags that always culminated in some tortured pun. Smith had created a holiday song sung to the tune of "The 12 Days of Christmas," and while I don't remember all the words, I'm pretty sure they included phrases such as "Kadish-a-tackling, Ferguson-a-passing, *Mick-a-Meyer* kicking on a Chuck Knox Super Bowl team."

We played TFL that snowy Christmas Eve afternoon as the temperature plummeted. At dusk I ventured over Pigeon Bridge to the now leveled Seneca Mall to buy a

Kenny Rogers' *Greatest Hits* album for my mother per her request, but wound up calling an audible and getting her one by Linda Ronstadt instead, which she later unappreciatively flung at me. On the table when I arrived home were two large pizza pies from Abbott Pizza, as tradition dictated, and I ate my slices while watching the "Happy Days" episode when Richie Cunningham happens upon The Fonz spending Christmas alone in the garage after claiming that he had plans to visit cousins in Waukesha.

Christmas Eve ruled, but Christmas Day itself had always been a letdown, even more so this year, because ironically my wish list had been mishandled and instead of receiving the record Kiss Alive II, as I had requested, I got two Kiss solo records, ones by Paul Stanley and Gene Simmons, neither of which did it for me (although there was one tune by Simmons, "Radioactive," that Shawn and I eventually grew to like). We got the usual bounty, as my father saw to it that some hockey equipment and a matching pair of railroad jackets emblazoned with the United Transportation Union logo awaited us under our beloved fake tree. Some people swear that there's nothing like a real tree, but I always felt that the ritual of dragging that thing out every year from the little "cubby hole" behind the mothball-scented closet at the top of our stairs was in a way its own uniquely special tradition.

Christmas Day of 1980 had been the coldest Buffalo had ever seen, with temperatures reaching 10-below. Even though Buffalo only averaged less than three sub-zero days a winter, much of the country had come to view the Queen City as American Siberia. In a story about the cold snap in the Northeast the following week, *Newsweek* magazine erroneously reported that on Christmas Day the thermometer in Buffalo had dipped to 29 degrees below zero. Pat Donlon from the Chamber of Commerce, perhaps emboldened by the success of the Talking Proud campaign, fired off a letter to *Newsweek*'s editors saying that not only had the magazine been 19 degrees off, but that the story at least should have pointed out that it had been the coldest December day in Buffalo history.

Because the arctic blast lingered, Knox packed up his team one week before the big playoff game in San Diego and traveled down to Vero Beach, Florida, to practice at Dodgertown, where the Los Angeles Dodgers held spring training. Vero Beach is on the east coast of Florida about halfway between Miami and Daytona Beach, and while many people hear "Vero Beach" and think of white hairs and yachties, that entire part of central Florida is rife with good old boys. When Jim Haslett read in the papers that there was a Ku Klux Klan presence nearby, he and Smerlas had the bright idea to put white pillowcases over their heads to try to scare two of the black players on the team, Frank Lewis and Reuben Gant (but neither of them bought the gag). An incident like that today might end up on HBO's *Real Sports* with Bryant Gumbel, but racial ribbing was part of the team dynamic back then. Buffalo itself was an extremely segregated town, but the Bills were united across color lines. Smerlas' best friend on the team after Haslett was Ben Williams. Jerry Butler was a popular character who was friends with everyone. Baby Johnson was equally loved. Even when the controversial Isiah Robertson found himself in a jam one late night in the wrong part of town, Lou Piccone was there to pull him out of it.

Running counter to all of this harmony however, was Robertson's impaired relationship with Jim Haslett. Despite publicly burying the hatchet (after the Steelers game the two linebackers posed for a picture with Haslett sticking his finger in his teammates mouth), they kept their distance from one another.

On the morning of New Year's Eve, a small Cocoa Beach newspaper printed a story in which Haslett freely discussed their scuffle and in the process bad-mouthed Robertson, calling him "the worst player on the team" and boasting that he'd "knocked the living [bleep] out of him."

Haslett insisted he'd been joking, but Robertson seemed upset, telling reporters the next day at Dodgertown that Haz had taken a "cheap shot" (which wouldn't have been the first) and that he had as many friends "as anybody on the team."

The dredging up of the Haslett/Robertson feud didn't prove to be a major distraction, no more so than the partying going on. Villapiano and Dobler were up to their boozing ways, hitting the bars in Vero Beach every night. When the team first arrived in town from Buffalo, all of the players had crowded on to a bus that was to take them to the Hilton, all of the players, that is, except Dobler and Villapiano, who'd rented themselves a tank-sized Lincoln Continental. They drove it straight to the Bamboo Room, a favorite haunt of Dobler's from his days attending New Orleans Saints camp held at Dodgertown.

Word had spread to Vero Beach that the Chargers were glad to be playing the Bills and not the Raiders, which served as motivational fodder for the Bills as they boarded the plane for San Diego on that second day of

1981. The Bills had already beaten the Chargers once that season, but only because of some exceptional special teams play and a few key bounces of the ball late in the game. No one was taking them lightly, but to the man the Bills believed they had the better team. On paper this was a matchup with perfect symmetry. The Chargers had the No. 1 offense; the Bills, the No. 1 defense. The Bills had allowed the fewest sacks (20) of any team, while the Chargers front four had registered a league-leading 60 sacks of opposing quarterbacks. One-fourth of the Bills sacks-allowed total had come in Week 5 courtesy of the Chargers, led by defensive tackles Gary Johnson and Louie Kelcher.

Most people believed this playoff game would come down to whether Cribbs, who had rushed for a season-high 128 yards in the muddy finale at Candlestick, could have another big game, not only because Ferguson's mobility was hampered, but more importantly, to keep Fouts off the field.

Fouts had one of the most dangerous arms in the game. He had averaged 300 yards per game passing during the season, though the Bills had held him to 214 in the earlier confrontation. But consider what the Bills were facing—possibly one of the most fearsome receiving trios ever assembled. Wide receivers John Jefferson and Charley Joiner, as well as mold-shattering tight end Kellen Winslow, *each* had 1,000 yards receiving during the season, an NFL first. The Chargers were only the second team in two decades to average 400 total yards per game. Play them in a nickel defense and the Chargers were inclined to run Chuck Muncie, who'd gained 128 yards in the Chargers season finale against the Steelers on *Monday Night Football* with the playoffs on the line. Muncie had been traded to the Chargers earlier in the season from the Saints. A runner-up to Archie Griffin in the 1975 Heisman Trophy race, Muncie had some productive seasons in New Orleans, including a 1,198-yard output in 1979. But a week after the Bills had held the Saints to 39 yards rushing, Muncie was benched by Saints coach Dick Nolan during a Week 4 loss against the Dolphins. Not long after that Muncie was traded to the Chargers. Against the Bills in Week 5, he'd rushed 10 times for just 37 yards.

Charger Coach Don Coryell was anticipating the Bills would key on the passing game, and planned to use Muncie often.

The game was at 4 P.M. on NBC. Sunny San Diego looked a million miles away to Buffalonians hunkered down for the long anticipated Saturday afternoon post-season showdown as the savage cold front continued to assault the region bringing with it blowing snow squalls. Record-low temperatures had been predicted and so people were being warned to stay indoors.

I had ventured out that day to the Seneca Mall to see the movie "Flash Gordon" for the second day in a row. I'd seen it the night before with Timmy Gallivan, Mikey Robertson and Brian George. I was absolutely blown away by that movie. Made in the U.K. by Mike Hodges, who'd been responsible for a hallmark of British cinema with his 1971 "Get Carter," "Flash Gordon" is probably best remembered by its theme song performed by Queen—*Flash! Ahhhhhhhh!* For my money (the General Cinema matinee was $1.75) it had everything I could have wanted in a movie. Talk about escapism. In this movie (honestly, it didn't seem lamely silly at the time) a football player for the New York Jets named Sam Jones (coincidentally played by never-again-heard-from actor Sam Jones), somehow hitches a ride to the planet Mongo with a mad scientist named Hans Zarkov (the singularly and weirdly named actor Topol of "Fiddler on the Roof" fame), where along with intrepid reporter Dale Arden (Melody Anderson), Flash encounters Ming the Merciless (Max von Sydow at his most unrecognizable since playing elderly Father Merrin in "The Exorcist"). There were lots of creatures and space battles, but it was all the extra little crazy stuff that captured my imagination: the Grizzly Adamsesque Prince Vultan and his flying hawkmen; the frightening suspense of the scene in which Flash and Prince Barin (Timothy Dalton) play a life or death game of chicken, reaching their hands into a hole-speckled heap of rock that is home to a poisonous eel-like creature; and of course, the super-sultry Princess Aura with those hypnotic eyes.

The empty, spotlit Seneca Mall parking lot and its chain of mountainous snowpiles served as a post-Flash adventureland for me and my friends that Friday night. On Saturday after delivering papers, I'd decided that the perfect way to get pumped for the upcoming Bills game was to see the movie again. It featured an ending I just had to experience one more time. For me, at that time, no other part of a movie had ever psyched me up as viscerally as this one had. In the scene, Flash Gordon, who had already overcome impossible trials and tribulations—defeating Ming, staving off galactic holocaust—comes up against one final remaining foe, a little floating robot sphere that seemed certain to laser him into oblivion. The camera angle is switched to that of the metallic nemesis, as if we the viewer were inside looking down on Flash, who is wielding a sword, but looking flustered. Then the hovering ball proclaims in typical staccato robotic fashion: "Congratulations Flash Gordon. You have saved your planet Earth."

Flash smiles, turns and drops his sword to the ground and then turns back around, jumping right up into the camera, right in our faces. He pumps his fist and yells "Yeah!" and the Queen music kicks in. Okay, I admit that while the goose bumps do not come as easily thinking about all that now, somehow then I considered a second helping of Flash Gordon as a perfect pre-game springboard.

I went by myself to the one o'clock show. Not only was I trying to reach back to double dip the enjoyment of the night before, I even tried to have repeat adventures on the giant snow mountain range in the parking lot, diving and falling from perilous angles, but really all I managed to do was to was to cover myself in snow. Caught up in my own little world, I must have lost track of the time. I knew the game would be starting soon and I had a ways to go to get home so I began the slow trudge home over the thruway to Ridge Road, under Pigeon Bridge, across the railroad tracks and through the backyards of Maryon Drive.

The wind was blowing and the thermometer was dropping quickly, down to 5 degrees with wind chills of minus 30. I remember I was freezing on that journey home, hoping I'd make it back in time for the start of the game. Apparently, a little kid completely covered in snow walking in dangerously cold, blizzard-like conditions on a highway overpass was enough to draw the attention of a complete stranger, a housewife in a station wagon, who abruptly pulled over and yelled at me (as if she were my mother), ordering me to get into the car.

Not quite sure what to do, I obeyed her command. Driving me home she scolded me ("Are you crazy?"), which was odd, because I didn't even know her. I gave her directions to my house, and as she pulled up in front, she looked at me with a knowing smile and said, "Oh, you're a Blake." I'm not sure if I thanked her, as I scampered out of the car and up my driveway, feeling a little bit foolish, but thankful I most certainly was, not only to be home safely and out of the cold, but more importantly, to be home in time for the kickoff.

I was alone in my basement watching the game. My brother Shawn was at hockey practice, having been picked to play on a special West Seneca All-Star team that would participate in a travel tournament. I wasn't happy about it. Our coach had mistakenly told me that I'd made the team. His assistant quickly corrected him, but dumbstruck by the news I was only half listening. "Well, one of you guys made it anyway," muttered the coach, a newly permed Jack Rubery. I should have known better. I played defense, and played well, but didn't have great speed or the wind required to put in consistently solid shifts. If I had been named an All-Star, well it must have been because of my smart, solid, always-in-position play. "Don't worry. You'll make it next year," I said sympathetically to my younger brother Shawn. But it was Shawn who made the team, not me.

The Bills received the opening kickoff. Dick Enberg and Merlin Olsen were calling the game, which featured the Bills in blue jerseys and white pants, and the Chargers in white shirts and yellow pants. On the fifth play of the game Ferguson went back to pass, finding himself swept up in the turmoil of the intense Chargers pass rush. Falling forward, Ferguson was hit by Louie Kelcher, who rolled over on Fergy's injured ankle, still tender beneath heavy tape. It twisted. Ferguson gritted his teeth and lay on the field as hearts across the Bills sideline and Western New York sank.

"Manucci!"

The sharp crackle of Knox's battle-intense command sent a chill down the back of the 23-year-old's neck. He was going in.

Ferguson's re-injury of his ankle had prompted a television timeout, during which just about every coach and player in earshot of Manucci had some words for the young backup. "Okay, here's the play," Knox said, and asked Manucci three times if he understood it. Prochaska was in his face, checking to see he had the play right also. "I-Right 21, you got that? I-Right 21." It was a simple hand-off to Cribbs. Manucci had it.

"Just make sure you get the snap clean," center Will Grant told him.

"Yeah, I got it," Manucci told him, feeling like maybe he was the only one left with any confidence in himself. One teammate clearly did not.

"Hey Manuch—keep your fuckin' ass in the pocket!" ordered Dobler as Manucci came into the huddle.

"Come on Connie, just let the kid play ball," said Reggie McKenzie, trying to establish calm.

After Cribbs darted for a couple of yards, Manucci, on third down and long, rolled out for what was supposed to be a simple screen pass to Curtis Brown, but he pump faked and turned it up field. Manucci couldn't believe his eyes—nothing but green to his right. He raced 18 yards for the first down into Chargers territory. A play later Manucci scrambled for another four yards, down to the Charger 27. But when he threw low to Roland Hooks on third down the improbable drive finally stalled. Still, Dan Manucci had gotten the Bills into field goal range. Mike-Mayer could tie it. Or not. His 44-yard field goal attempt smacked off the uprights.

If Manucci stayed in the game even five plays that day it was only because Bills trainers Eddie Abramoski and Bud Tice couldn't re-tape Ferguson's ankle fast enough. On the sidelines, Knox had given the order, and despite the pain, Ferguson's attitude was that as long as he didn't have to run around much he could suck it up and throw off his other foot.

The Bills were trailing 3-0. Fergy limped back out on the field for the next series and moved with the measured steps of a fastwalker. Ferguson was effective despite the pain, which only grew worse under the extra-tight tape job. He led the Bills on a quarter-chewing, 72-yard, 12-play drive that ended with Leaks going straight up the gut for the touchdown from the one-yard line. The Bills had the lead, 7–3.

Late in the first half Fouts aired one out for Charley Joiner but the Bills' Charlie Romes came with a heavy lick, knocking the ball loose. Bill Simpson recovered the fumble in Chargers territory. The courageous Ferguson, wincing with every step, went right to work. He hit Frank Lewis with an 18-yard pass to the 11. Then, throwing off balance and awkwardly from his back foot, hit Lewis again a play later for a 9-yard touchdown pass with 16 seconds left in the half. Going into the locker room the Bills led 14–3. Destiny, it seemed, was on their side.

At half time Ferguson's ankle was re-taped yet again, and the Bills were feeling confident. In the Chargers locker room things were silent, though in the second half they came out swinging.

It took Fouts just four plays to get the Chargers back in the game. First, a handoff to Muncie for 18 yards. Then, Joiner beat cornerback Mario Clark for a 45-yard catch down to the 7. One play later, Fouts fired a pass to Joiner for the touchdown. Any feeling that the Bills were going to waltz into the AFC Championship had disappeared barely a minute into the half.

Still, the Bills had plenty of chances to seize control of the contest. It looked like they had done so when special teams ace Lou Piccone blocked a Rick Partridge punt to give the Bills the ball on the Charger 38 with seven minutes left in the third quarter. The Bills moved the ball down to the Chargers 24. But Ferguson was intercepted by Glen Edwards at the nine after overthrowing Roland Hooks.

Later in the third quarter, Ferguson connected with Lewis on a 43-yard pass down to the Charger 21. But the play was called back because of a holding penalty on Ken Jones. On the next play Ferguson, barely able to plant, was sacked for a 10-yard loss. He shrugged off the pain and pulled himself up.

The Chargers kicked a field goal to make it 14–13 and appeared to be on the verge of taking the lead in the fourth quarter when Fouts got picked off by Simpson playing in man coverage. The throw was intended for barely-used, little-known backup receiver Ron Smith, an ex-Ram. During the regular season, Smith, in 15 games after coming over from Los Angeles, had caught just four passes for 48 yards.

The ball bounced off Smith's cobwebbed hands and landed in Simpson's clutches as he fell out of bounds at

the Bills 7-yard line with 9 minutes left. Simpson's interception appeared to have just put this one away. But the
Bills couldn't move the ball. Knowing Ferguson was
practically immobile, Coryell's plan to key on Cribbs
had worked. The Chargers lined up to receive a punt
with about six minutes to play.

Return man Mike Fuller was heading upfield when he
was nailed by Ervin Parker. He fumbled—recovered by
the Bills at the Charger 39! Now the Bills could finally
rest easy. All of the tension and uncertainty drifted away
as the clock ticked and the Bills scratched out another 9
yards down to the 30-yard line.

*The Bills were going to be one game away from the Super
Bowl.*

One more first down and the Bills could take a knee.
Ferguson handed off to Cribbs who was set deep in the
backfield. But Cribbs was thrown for a one-yard loss by
titanic defensive end Fred Dean. The Chargers had
stopped him, just as they had all day, just as their game
plan had dictated.

On fourth-and two, with 3:59 left and the Bills in a position to potentially get one more first down and run out
the clock, Knox instead went for the field goal. Mike-
Mayer's 49-yard attempt fell short.

Uh-oh.

Suddenly the Chargers had new life. Fouts picked up
a first down to the Chargers 48 with a pass to Jefferson.
One play later, on second down and 10, Fouts dispatched
another pass to Jefferson, this one a poorly-timed duck
floating toward the sideline. Romes turned and darted in
front of the veteran Charger receiver for the sure interception. Except Romes dropped the ball. It bounced right

off his chest. Had Romes extended his hands, the game would have been over.

Now it was third and 10. There was 2:08 to play. If the Bills could just hold the Chargers here they would have to go for it on fourth down, as a field goal was out of the question. The Bills would be a mere one play away from the AFC Championship. Fouts dropped back to pass. And that's when it happened, out of nowhere, without warning, like a savage bolt of lightning. Charger lightning.

The highly potent Charger offensive weapons were parceled out across the field, a formidable spread formation of Jefferson, Joiner and Winslow on the left; on the far right, the sparingly used Ron Smith.

The Bills blitzed Fouts with their outside linebackers, Sanford and Robertson, while dispensing double coverage on both Jefferson and Joiner. The lone Charger back was Mike Smith. He was the responsibility of strong safety Steve Freeman. Bill Simpson, the red-bearded free safety, was in "Red Dog" coverage—man coverage, specifically the man on the right side of the field. Ron Smith was all his. Just a few minutes earlier, in the same coverage, Simpson had gotten himself what seemed like the game-winning interception.

Smith knew Simpson well enough from their days together on the Rams. While Simpson had gotten the better of him on that last pass, it wasn't likely to happen again. Smith had run a hundred post patterns on this guy in practice. Smith didn't think Simpson could cover him man-to-man with this much wide open space. Neither did Fouts.

The ball traveled about 40 yards in the air with the brisk zip of a first-down strike, so there wasn't time to wonder how this would turn out.

Smith ran his post, juking outside and then quickly turning inside with the middle of the field his for taking. Simpson waited one second too long to break for the ball which landed in Smith's hands right around the twenty-yard line. Slipping as he dove, Simpson tried desperately to grab Smith's right leg. He missed it by inches. There was now a clear path to the end zone. Freeman, who was supposed to help Simpson when the running back stayed in to block, was already scrambling to get back. In fact, the pass had sailed no more than a few inches over his outstretched hands on route to Smith. There was no stopping him. He raced untouched for a touchdown. The Chargers led 20–14.

The Ron Smith touchdown came like a sucker punch to the face. Unexpected, devastating. Simpson remained collapsed on the field where Smith had left him. He watched the celebration of the Chargers, his eyes gazing up to the end zone seats where just months earlier he had been sitting carefree, a mere mortal.

In the darkness of my basement I shuddered, and collapsed on the couch in a ball of denial. Even though the Bills still had a chance to regain the lead, the terror of knowing that perhaps there was no tomorrow suddenly had become all-consuming. Right then I knew the perilous downside of this deal.

So I hoped against hope. I watched, though I couldn't watch. My stomach burned and I felt the despair growing. I watched Ferguson hobble back on to the field, barely able to walk. I watched him throw a pass to Frank Lewis to the Bills 48. I watched and prayed, and cried, and yelled to the heavens "Please God!" and then I saw, in the darkness of my basement, Fergy, barely able to place any weight on that left foot, throw one deep for

Jerry Butler. And as it sailed high, out of Butler's reach and into the awaiting arms of Chargers defensive back Glen Edwards, I watched the best Bills season ever come crashing to an end.

In the locker room the Bills were utterly devastated, no one more so than Simpson, who sat beside his locker with his head down. Knox, seeing the inconsolable gaze, grabbed Simpson and said, "Listen, Billy, we'd never have even gotten to the playoffs without you."

As Bills owner Ralph Wilson left the stadium, someone from the Chargers organization kindly shouted, "We're just lucky you guys didn't have a quarterback with two good legs." Wilson smiled, stung as he was by the bitter loss. He'd never been more proud of a player than he was of Joe Ferguson.

I don't know how I endured that defeat. That night Timmy Gallivan came to my back door and we ventured out into the frozen air to try to get on with our lives and do what came naturally—go hang out on Abbott Road.

Man, was it cold, and the Bills defeat made it feel even colder. Shortly before 9 P.M., the National Weather Service reported that the temperature at the Greater Buffalo International Airport had dipped to one below zero, breaking the old record of zero set for that date in Buffalo on January 3, 1904.

I still clearly remember that blustery Saturday night. I can see this older, delinquent kid named Bill Faltisco, who always carried around with him a huge boom box, which that night seemed to continuously blare Queen's "Another One Bites the Dust" with all of its bass-thumping roller-skating party anthem splendor. We seventh graders—myself, Timmy Gallivan, Mikey Robertson, Tommy McDonnell, John Fischer, Pat Keane,

Moose Moreales—freely mixed with the eighth graders, guys we looked up to, like Brian Milligan, Chris Fischer, Johnny Novak, Dennis Sands, Chuckie Long and Mike Dwyer. They'd come down to our turf. We stood in front of Abbott Pizza on the corner of Abbott Road and Densmore, hitching on the bumpers of cars down icy side streets, pelting 14-A city buses and eighth grade girls with snowballs, all the while commiserating over the sad outcome of the game.

"I thought for sure we were going to win," I told Timmy Gallivan.

He did too.

EPILOGUE

In the early summer of 1981, Morley Safer, a CBS television reporter best known for his work on the acclaimed news magazine *60 Minutes*, noticed he was getting a lot of mail from Buffalo—an awful lot of mail. The letters were angry, some even nasty, and Safer didn't understand the virulent response to what he believed was a harmless crack.

On Monday, June 8, 1981, Safer did a segment, not on *60 Minutes*, but on the *CBS Morning News*, in which the checkered-shirt-wearing correspondent took a satirical swipe at four chefs from mainland China who were learning American-style cooking at Buffalo's new waterfront Hilton. The hotel had just been built by San Francisco developer Clement Chen. Finding the concept wonderfully juxtaposed, Safer riffed that the hotel was on the "more than aromatic shores of Lake Erie" and that the project would surely become "an exercise in international ill-will."

A firestorm of rebuttals erupted from the Buffalo media. Local CBS affiliate Channel 4 reporter Kevin O'-Connell took strong issue with the remarks on the air and demanded that Safer apologize. Erie County Executive Ed Rutkowski wrote a heartfelt letter to the Editor of the *Courier-Express* that summed up the way a lot of people felt.

"We who live here in Buffalo and Erie County don't

need the approval of Morley Safer or CBS to appreciate what we have," Rutkowski wrote. "We are proud of our industrial past. The muscle of our industry and labor, and the genius of our commerce, helped build and protect this nation."

By the time Safer received his estimated 2,000[th] letter from Buffalo supporters, he realized that perhaps he did take a cheap shot. He had to respect such indomitable civic pride.

Courier-Express publisher Roger Parkinson, in conjunction with the Chamber of Commerce, extended an invitation to Safer to visit Buffalo. Later that summer, Safer, to his credit, graciously accepted, though it is believed that Safer was quietly nudged by CBS Television President Gene Jankowski, who as it turned out, was a Buffalo native. Jankowski accompanied Safer to Buffalo that day.

"This whole thing started in fun and I was determined not to apologize," Safer told a crowd gathered outside One M&T Plaza for a special noon rally. "But after one of the most gracious mornings of my life I must say, I am sorry."

Safer hadn't even been to Buffalo for the original piece, and conceded that it had been years since he'd last had occasion to visit. It was no boom town, but Buffalo was on the rise, even Safer had to admit. Downtown was experiencing a reawakening. There was a newly built convention center and three new hotels, not to mention a 6-mile long light rail transit system under construction, certainly not the New York City subway, but the area's largest public works project in decades. Steel and auto industries were still depressed, but light and medium manufacturing was surviving, while the area banking industry was growing as the Reagan bull market, still a year away from its liftoff, took form. The region's educational offerings, UB and nearby RIT in Rochester, also enjoyed national recognition. So all of this, combined with the tourism potential of Niagara Falls and Niagara on the Lake, proved that city leaders were right: there was plenty to be proud of in Buffalo.

The Bills, meanwhile, kept their winning ways alive. The team came back from San Diego to a hero's welcome. Thousands gathered at the airport to greet them in weather barely fit for the parameters of human endurance. Bill Simpson, who'd felt about as low as the frightening wind chill factor, found solace in his teammates' support.

Joe Ferguson, who had been told all along that his ankle was badly sprained, later found out from doctors that the ankle, in fact, was broken.

The Chargers would go on to lose the AFC Championship at home to the Raiders, a team the Bills had decimated earlier that season. A wildcard team, the Tom Flores-coached Raiders would have had to travel to Rich Stadium had Ron Smith not shattered the Bills season. But instead they went down the coast to San Diego where they beat the Chargers 34–27 en route to a Super Bowl victory over Ron Jaworski's Eagles. The Raiders became the first wildcard team to ever claim the Lombardi Trophy. Quarterback Jim Plunkett was named MVP; the game's most memorable play was Kenny King's 80-yard touchdown off a screen pass.

History has mostly forgotten the '80 Bills defense but the Bermuda Triangle and company finished the season with high honors. Not only had they allowed the fewest total yards, but they allowed the fewest first downs, not to mention the fewest yards per play. Only two teams, the Eagles and the Oilers, gave up fewer points.

On offense, Joe Cribbs was named Rookie of the Year. Only Oiler superstar Earl Campbell rushed for more yards than Cribbs in 1980. Operating out of the shotgun, just the second team ever to do so, the Bills led the league in third-down conversions. Discounting the Week 15 Patriots game in which raw quarterbacks Dan Manucci and David Humm were sacked eight times, the Bills offensive line averaged well under one sack per game during the regular season.

Chuck Knox was named Coach of the Year by *The Associated Press*.

With the Bills first pick, Knox drafted Penn State fullback Booker Moore. Weeks into camp, Moore was diagnosed with a rare disease that attacks the nervous system, and missed the entire season.

The Bills opened up the 1981 season with back-to-back blowouts, over the Jets (31–0) and the Colts (35–3) before dropping a disappointing game to the NFC Champion Eagles during a special Thursday Night edition of *Monday Night Football*. The season took a nosedive, Fergy began throwing interceptions in batches of four per game, and it appeared in Week 12 the Bills would surely miss the playoffs, trailing the Patriots at Rich Stadium 17–13 on their own 27 with 30 seconds on the clock and no timeouts. A loss would bring their record to 6–6.

On first down Ferguson laid one out at midfield for Roland Hooks, in for the injured Joe Cribbs. Hooks made as spectacular a diving catch as there has ever been, one in which his full body had to be extended as far as it could just to get his fingertips on the pigskin. Fergy quickly threw the ball out of bounds stopping the clock with 12 seconds left. Time for one play, Big Ben, and as time ticked down, Ferguson's prayer of a pass sailed through the chilly November evening. The few thousand fans still on hand, still believing, watched, utterly stupefied, as the ball careened past the outstretched hands of six Patriots, off the fingers of Pats linebacker Mike Hawkins and into the awaiting arms of lifelong Bills backup Roland Hooks. "How do you spell relief?" Channel 7's Rick Azar asked later on the air in a play on of the Rolaids commercial. "R-O-L-A-N-D!"

The Bills won their next three games, securing a wild-card playoff berth. That wildcard game, played at Shea Stadium a few days after Christmas, saw Charles Romes recover a Bruce Harper fumble on the opening kickoff for a touchdown as the Bills sprinted to a 24–0 first half lead. But the Jets came back. Driving for the winning touchdown with a few seconds left, Jets quarterback Richard Todd was intercepted in the Bills end zone in one of the most heart wrenching, yet ultimately glorious games Bills fans had ever witnessed. And the man who secured the Bills first playoff win in 16 years with that saving interception was none other than Bill Simpson.

The '81 season predictably came to yet another heart-breaking culmination the following week in Cincinnati. With three minutes left and down 28–21, Ferguson led the Bills to the Bengal 20 and appeared to have gotten a crucial fourth-down conversion when Lou Piccone caught a six-yard sideline pass. But Ferguson got the play off a half-second too late and the Bills were penalized for delay of game. He overthrew Hooks on the next play. Another season had come to an end with Bills fans left wondering, "If only . . ."

In 1982, the Bills opened 2–0, including a stirring 23–22

Week 2 comeback victory against the Vikings on yet another ABC Thursday night game. The now primetime-worthy Bills trailed at one point 19–0, but Ferguson capped the rally with a touchdown pass to Jerry Butler. The following week the NFL players went on strike, and by the time it was settled and the season resumed (Nov. 21), the Bills had lost momentum. They went on to lose the last three games of the strike-abbreviated season to finish 4–5.

Plans to take the Talking Proud campaign national were shelved, and a new campaign, "Buffalo, You're Looking Good," took its place, but it just wasn't the same.

The following January, Chuck Knox resigned as coach of the Bills to become head coach of the Seattle Seahawks. Earlier that month, Dr. Jerry Argovitz, agent to Bills star running back Joe Cribbs and backer of the USFL's Houston Gamblers, told reporters he would do whatever it took to evacuate Cribbs out of Buffalo. Cribbs would eventually leave for the USFL's Birmingham Stallions.

Quarterbacks coach Kay Stephenson took over for Knox as head coach. That spring, using a pick obtained by trading Tom Cousineau to the Browns, the Bills selected University of Miami quarterback Jim Kelly. Later, Kelly signed with Argovitz's Gamblers, who agreed to pay him a salary in the neighborhood of $1 million per year, making him the upstart league's second-highest paid player behind Herschel Walker, as the age of truly enormous NFL salaries began to unfurl.

The Bills finished 8–8 in 1983. The following year the Bills would go 2–14. Late that season, Ferguson was benched. His replacement, Joe Dufek. The following spring Fergy, who'd played 12 seasons and 168 games, would be traded to the Lions. Before he left town Ferguson told reporters: "I want to be remembered as a guy who tried."

Coached by Hank Bullough and quarterbacked by Vince Ferragamo, the Bills finished the 1985 season 2–14, their second straight two-win season. While it was impossible to imagine at the time, there was light at the end of the tunnel. For many years to come Bills fans would enjoy a level of football glory rarely ever contemplated by Western New Yorkers, and, ironically, a level of football agony equally as unimaginable.

Buffalo bashing is as prevalent now as it was in the 1970s, if not worse.

Once, a movie reviewer named John Boonstra, writing in 1997 about Vincent Gallo's "Buffalo '66," opened his column with the rhetorical question: "Is there an American city so synonymous with urban decay as Buffalo?"

"There it sits," Boonstra continued. "In the armpit formed by Canada's border with New York. It gets the meanest snowfalls east of the Rockies. It's home to the losingest Super Bowl contenders in history. And as anyone who's driven through it en route to happier places will attest, it looks bad."

He went on to give Gallo's movie four stars.

And the beatdown goes on. And on.

This past July, as the newly unlocked NHL held its draft lottery, Rich Ackerman, one of the newscasters on WFAN's "Mike and the Mad Dog," was discussing with host Mike Francesa the fate of Canadian hockey phenom Sidney Crosby. Francesa held out hopes that the teenage star, and potential hockey savior, would wind up in major market New York.

Ackerman chimed in bluntly, "With the NHL's luck Crosby will wind up in Buffalo."

If Buffalo does have a persecution complex, it's probably not unwarranted. The city has become something a national fat kid who gets rocks thrown at him because it's the thing to do.

These days as Buffalo struggles with yet another dismal economic chapter—a staggering Erie County budget crisis, control boards, all while having had to endure a winter without the Sabres—there is little doubt the city will pull through. Just as certain, the national knocks on Buffalo, the cheap shots, will continue unabated. Maybe if the Bills ever somehow won the Super Bowl, maybe one day the town could be vindicated, if only briefly. Or then again maybe one day Ralph Wilson's heirs will sell the Bills, and the franchise will be moved away, to a more beautiful, warmer city, and then surely all of the wisecracking pundits will be able to really tease Buffalo, which from their high horses will surely be seen as having nothing left.

And if the Bills are uprooted (such a calamity would undoubtedly have to transgress over more than a few dead bodies) well, my guess is that Buffalo would survive. What choice would there be?

All the PR campaigns in the world could never convey why Buffalonians take so much pride in their hometown. The reason is simple: Good-hearted people who care more about one another than about what anybody thinks of them.

—July 25, 2005

www.ingramcontent.com/pod-product-compliance
Lightning Source LLC
Chambersburg PA
CBHW031836090426
42741CB00005B/264